REALITY TV

From early first-wave programs such as *Candid Camera*, *An American Family*, and *The Real World* to the shows on our television screens and portable devices today, reality television consistently takes us to cities—such as New York, Los Angeles, and Boston—to imagine the place of urbanity in American culture and society. Jon Kraszewski offers the first extended account of this phenomenon, as he makes the politics of urban space the center of his history and theory of reality television.

Kraszewski situates reality television in a larger economic transformation that started in the 1980s when America went from an industrial economy, when cities were home to all classes, to its post-industrial economy as cities became key points in a web of global financing, expelling all economic classes except the elite and the poor. Reality television in the industrial era reworked social relationships based on class, race, and gender for liberatory purposes, which resulted in an egalitarian ethos in the genre. However, reality television of the post-industrial era attempts to convince viewers that cities still serve their interests, even though most viewers find city life today economically untenable. Each chapter uses a key theoretical concept from spatial theory—such as power geometries, diasporic nostalgia, orientalism, the imagination of social expulsions, and the relationship between the country and the city—to illuminate the way reality television engages this larger transformation of urban space in America.

Jon Kraszewski is Associate Professor and Program Coordinator of Visual and Sound Media at Seton Hall University. He is author of the book *The New Entrepreneurs: An Institutional History of Television Anthology Writers* (Wesleyan, 2010), as well as numerous articles on television and film.

Routledge Television Guidebooks

The Routledge Television Guidebooks offer an introduction to and overview of key television genres and formats. Each guidebook contains an introduction, including a brief history; defining characteristics and major series; key debates surrounding themes, formats, genres, and audiences; questions for discussion; and a bibliography of further reading and watching.

Science Fiction TV
J. P. Telotte

Political TV
Chuck Tryon

Lifestyle TV
Laurie Ouellette

The Sitcom
Jeremy Butler

Reality TV
Jonathan Kraszewski

REALITY TV

JON KRASZEWSKI

Routledge
Taylor & Francis Group

NEW YORK AND LONDON

First published 2017
by Routledge
711 Third Avenue, New York, NY 10017

and by Routledge
2 Park Square, Milton Park, Abingdon, Oxon OX14 4RN

Routledge is an imprint of the Taylor & Francis Group, an informa business

Library of Congress Cataloging in Publication Data
Names: Kraszewski, Jon.
Title: Reality TV / Jon Kraszewski.
Description: New York, NY : Routledge, 2017.
Identifiers: LCCN 2016050430| ISBN 9780415741972
    (hardback) | ISBN 9780415741989 (pbk.)
Subjects: LCSH: Reality television programs—United
    States—History and criticism.
Classification: LCC PN1992.8.R43 K75 2017 | DDC
    791.45/6—dc23
LC record available at https://lccn.loc.gov/2016050430

ISBN: 978-0-415-74197-2 (hbk)
ISBN: 978-0-415-74198-9 (pbk)
ISBN: 978-1-315-81495-7 (ebk)

Typeset in Joanna MT Std
by Swales & Willis Ltd, Exeter, Devon, UK

Printed by CPI on sustainably sourced paper

To My Quack Pack:
Barbara, Lanny, Leo, Oliver, and Sue Kraszewski—
For giving me the best life possible
And to The Quack Pack:
Dan, Danielle, Ian, Shane, and Britney—
For giving me the best season of reality television possible

CONTENTS

FIGURES

ACKNOWLEDGMENTS

I am grateful to Victoria E. Johnson for recommending that I write for the Routledge Television Guidebooks series. I feel lucky to have worked with Erica Wetter, my editor at Routledge. Her suggestions on what programs to analyze and her enthusiasm for the project kept me going. I am grateful for support at Seton Hall University. The Office of the Provost granted me a sabbatical and a course release so that I could first start and then finish this book. The University Research Council awarded me a Summer Stipend during my early stages of writing. As chair, Thomas Rondinella approved a sabbatical for this book. Deirdre Yates, who became my chair and then my dean, supported my course release and was understanding of the time I needed to write. Dean Yates and Assistant Dean Christine Krus provided generous funding for the images for this book. Chris Sharrett gave me great advice and kept me laughing. I am also grateful for good friends who supported me throughout this project. Blair Bromfield provided childcare and offered support often during the final stages of writing. Gwendolyn Foster offered constant encouragement. Wheeler Winston Dixon supported my work on reality television. My family has been wonderful. My dad and mom, Lanny and Barbara Kraszewski, were willing to drive across Pennsylvania and provide childcare on a moment's notice, and my mom always shared her extensive knowledge about reality television. My kids, Leo and Oliver, made me happy, understood when I needed to write, and watched *Survivor*, *The Amazing Race*, *Big Brother*, and *American Ninja Warrior* with me. To Sue Kraszewski, thanks for everything. You are amazing. I love you more than I love *The Real Housewives*. Lucky, Alice, and GoGo Kraszewski were faithful writing companions from start to finish. Thanks to Linda and Tom Pavlesich for providing childcare during the final weekend of writing. As this is a book for undergraduate readers, I would like to thank students in my reality television courses at Seton Hall who offered valuable feedback on ideas in this project and always made it enjoyable for me to teach this television genre. Thanks also to my favorite undergraduate professors at IUP— my mom, Ken Wilson, Joe Krupnik, Irwin Marcus, and Wendy Carse—who taught me how great undergraduate education can be.

AUTHOR'S BIOGRAPHY

Jon Kraszewski is Associate Professor and Program Coordinator of Visual and Sound Media in the College of Communication and the Arts at Seton Hall University in South Orange, New Jersey. *The New Entrepreneurs: An Institutional History of Television Anthology Writers*, his first book, was published by Wesleyan University Press in 2010. His articles have appeared in journals such as *Quarterly Review of Film and Video, Journal of Sport and Social Issues, Popular Communication: The International Journal of Media and Culture, Journal of Film and Video, and The Velvet Light Trap*. He also has chapters in anthologies such as *Extreme Weather and Global Media* (eds. Julia Leyda and Diane Negra. Routledge, 2015) and *Reality TV: Remaking Television Culture* (eds. Susan Murray and Laurie Ouellette. New York University Press, 2009).

INTRODUCTION

Scan the listing of reality television programs on your television menu or using your favorite media app. There's a good chance the list of shows you see will feature city life. Many reality programs, in fact, are named after a city or a city neighborhood—like *Baldwin Hills* (2007–09), *The Hills* (short for the Hollywood Hills, 2006–10), and *The City* (a reference to Manhattan, 2008–10). In addition, television channels frequently use cities as the primary way to differentiate series within a successful reality television franchise. For example, Bravo's *Real Housewives* franchise has a New York City series (2008–present), an Atlanta series (2008–present), a Washington, DC series (2010), a Beverly Hills series (2010–present), and a Miami series (2011–13), to name but a few. E!'s Kardashian franchise has numerous spin-offs based in specific cities such as *Kourtney and Khloe Take Miami* (2009–10), *Kourtney and Kim Take Miami* (2013), and *Kourtney and Kim Take New York* (2011–12). *The Real World* (1992–present) categorizes its seasons not by number, but by location (the San Francisco season, the Boston season, the Seattle season, the Chicago season, etc.). Several reality real-estate programs such as *House Hunters* (1999–present), *Flip This House* (2005–09), and *Rehab Addict* (2010–present) fixate on the market of a particular city for an episode or for the series. Other programs such as *Selling New York* (2010–present) and *Selling Los Angeles* (2011–present) highlight their city locales in the title.

The reality gameshow *The Amazing Race* (2001–present) sets most episodes in cosmopolitan cities throughout the world. Even programs set in tropical locations, such as *Survivor* (2000–present), call on American urban culture by casting characters such as Boston Rob, who base their identity on a specific city. While we typically watch programs about the city's wealthiest residents, some programs such as *Vanderpump Rules* (2013–present) show us the lives of urban servers—people who provide a service.

As these shows illustrate, city life is a central part of reality television; however, reality television scholarship has yet to address this phenomenon.[1] So, the goal of this book is to understand the history of reality television within a larger context of economic history, urban demography, and the social relationships constructed within city spaces. One broad question guides this book: why has city life become the defining feature of reality television at exactly the same moment that urban living has become untenable for most Americans? This contradiction surfaces in the twenty-first century, where Americans seem to experience two different worlds of city life. The first world, the one on reality television, is an enjoyable world—a world of upbeat montages where beautiful images of the city pulsate to the lively beat of pop music. It's a world in which people seemingly do well and can achieve the American dream of economic class mobility, a world in which rich people are fun and seem, in some ways, to mirror the identities of the rest of us. And then there are the real cities, cities that sociologist Saskia Sassen argues operate in a brutal political economy of social expulsions. Sassen claims "the past two decades have seen a sharp growth in the number of people, enterprises, and places expelled from the core social and economic orders of our time."[2] Income inequality no longer captures class differences in global capitalism. Now social groups are eradicated from certain areas; the city is one such area. As the world economy becomes based on extreme zones of profit extraction, global cities—centers of finance such as New York, Los Angeles, Chicago, and Boston—become centers of wealth while areas of outsourced work become spaces of extreme poverty. As a result, cities have become home to two types of residents: the extremely wealthy and the extremely poor. The city is a space for the elite and their servant class. Gentrification, a rising cost of living, and new economies have expelled the other classes from America's global cities.

At the very least, the new global economy means most of us aren't realistically planning to move to America's global cities. But why do so many of us constantly return to a place on reality television that we cannot return to in real life? What is the relationship between the city of reality television, which we seem to love, and the city in the political economy of social expulsions, which has more than likely evicted someone we know—a family member, friend, acquaintance, or even ourselves? When we ask these questions, we are bringing space out of the background of our television texts and placing it in the foreground. Space is no longer an insignificant part of the mise-en-scene where action takes place. It's not even a central character in a show, just as important as the other cast members. Rather, space becomes a set of social, economic, and cultural relationships mapped onto a particular place. We can think of this as a three-layered model. When we live in society, we are shaped by the way legal, medical, educational, religious, governmental, and economic institutions construct ideas about aspects of our identities such as class, gender, race, sex, nation, region, disability, etc. We also live in a certain place, such as a town, city, region, and nation. Spatial relationships are the ways that institutional constructs of our identities are mapped onto a particular place. Inspired by geographer Doreen Massey, I treat space as the geographic coordinates of social power within a given place. The ramifications of this are that space is never a given. It's never a set of a priori relationships. Space is always under construction by institutions and people looking to define it in their interests.

When we think about the fun and pleasurable city spaces of reality television, it should quickly become apparent that spatial relationships on reality television are not simply a mirror of the spatial relationships within real global cities. Rather, the stories, visuals, characters, and sounds of contemporary urban reality shows help us imagine what contemporary cities mean to us. In his landmark book *The Image of the City*, Kevin Lynch introduces the notion of *urban imageability*: "the quality in a physical object which gives it a high probability of evoking a strong image in a given observer."[3] We create mental maps of what cities *mean* to us. Postmodern theorist Frederic Jameson added to Lynch's theory when he coined the phrase *cognitive mapping*, a process that places subjective and political aspects onto our imaging of the city.[4] We might not physically inhabit televisual space the way we inhabit real urban space, but television programs help us cognitively map cities. They attempt to move us to certain social, cultural, political, and economic notions of what a city should be and who it should serve. Thus, when we look at the joyous, upbeat city of reality television, it's not that it is oblivious to the political economy of social expulsions. Rather, it is offering an array of aesthetic, narrative, and characterological strategies to shape our imagination of contemporary urbanity.

Spatial theorist Henri Lefebvre's argument that space is constructed hegemonically to serve the interests of the ruling class can help us see the relationship between real life and reality television cities.[5] *Hegemony* is a theory of social control whereby power is exerted not through blunt force but through winning consent of the oppressed. Institutions with the power to control society—medical, legal, educational, governmental, and entertainment institutions—create a loose network of control and offer various arguments for people with less social power to accept a view of society that serves the ruling class. So if we bring this approach to reality television, the pleasurable cities in the genre aren't bluntly forcing the political economy of expulsions on us. Rather, they are making arguments, very subtle at times, to let us know that the era of social expulsions isn't that bad. In fact, the programs make it seem like the contemporary cityscape is serving the interests of all of us in order to direct our attention away from the city serving the interests of the elite.

Reality television uses many aesthetic strategies to present today's cities, the cities of the political economy of social expulsions; however, many of the identities, plots, and sounds we encounter on contemporary urban reality shows recall older moments in urban history when the city was home to all classes. This strategy—*time shifting*—allows the viewer to embrace the contemporary global city. Raymond Williams' theory of dominant, residual, and emerging cultures provides a useful language to think about how this works. For Williams, historical moments are neither static nor self-contained. They consist of dominant ideas secured through social and political organizations as well as through fictions. Dominant ideas are contested by (1) residual ideas that have been replaced but still have lasting effects on society, and (2) emerging ideas that suggest new ways to organize society.[6] These terms—*dominant* and *residual*—are valuable for understanding how past ideas frequently haunt present texts, but there need not be such an antago-nistic relationship between the residual and the dominant. Often the resid-ual activates a sense of nostalgia for the past. The word *nostalgia* comes from two Greek words—*nostos* (homecoming) and *algos* (longing). Seeing residual urban identities on reality television frequently activates a longing within us for the way things used to be, for a time when the city could house more classes than just the elite and those who serve them. But the time-shifting of reality television—the ability to sprinkle older urbanisms within the new city—reworks the nature of longing, making it seem like the new city con-tinues to serve as our old home. As Chapter Two will show, we don't long for full-scale recreations of early twentieth-century cities; we cognitively map the spaces of the twenty-first-century city by imagining them through residual urban tropes that still appeal to our interests.

Another strategy for winning our consent for the political economy of expulsions is to normalize the city as home to the elite; this occurs by con-trasting the elite with social groups constructed as "others." Chapter Three offers an extended view of this othering process, but for now it is important to note, generally, that *othering* is a practice whereby a group with social power imagines another group with less social power to be lacking key qualities of a narrowly defined view of humanity. This disempowered social group has a different raced, classed, gendered, or national identity than the group in power, and their difference is not understood on its own terms. It is constructed as somehow abnormal and contrasted with the dominant group's normality. Just visualizing the urban elite on the screen might make their interests seem antithetical to our own, but if reality programs use a socially disempowered group to create an other, then the elite take on a normal quality to which we can consent.

The argument of this book is not simply that urban reality television programs help to win viewers' consent for the political economy of social expulsions. Rather, I aim for an argument larger in scope: reality television has gone from offering an open construction of urban spatial relations in the twentieth century to winning our consent of closed spatial relationships in the twenty-first century. Rather than opening oppressive spatial relations in cities, twenty-first-century reality television merely makes it seem like the city is open to residual notions of economic mobility and residual urban identities to assuage our feelings of social injustices found in the political economy of urban expulsions. Reality television has gone from a genre that challenged spatial relationships for liberatory and utopian purposes to a genre that helps to assert the dominant spatial relationships of our time. In making this argument, I bring together abstract theories of space from Marxist and cultural geography with concrete urban economics from sociology to define the terms *open* and *closed spaces*.

OPEN AND CLOSED SPACES IN THEORY, IN URBAN ECONOMIES, AND ON REALITY TELEVISION

I use the term *open space* to mean two things: that spatial relationships within a place are open to liberatory change and that the places themselves have spatial relationships that make them open to residents of various classes. I am indebted to Marxist geographer Doreen Massey for the first point. Massey believed in the rights of the socially oppressed to change relationships within space in order to live with dignity, but it is important to note that her Marxism was shaped by the work of Louis Althusser. Althusser broke away from Marx's teleological view of history that claimed society was on a predetermined path where the proletariats (the workers) would revolt and overthrow the bourgeoisie (the ruling class and elite) in order to create a classless society based on equality. He argued that nothing was a given in history and that all aspects of society could be challenged and reworked. Massey used this point to claim that space can always be contested and structured differently, since space is always in a process of formation and never finished. The implications of this are that spatial relationships are defined by multiplicities. Although a dominant group can shape spatial relationships for their interests, other social groups challenge them and offer competing ways to structure society within a space. Space is made through hegemonic forces trying to convince people to accept the dominant views and counterhegemonic forces, which attempt to shape spatial relationships to liberate the oppression of the socially disempowered. By drawing on Massey, we can see how space is open to reinterpretation and reorganization.

The second point I make about openness is based on urban demography, not theories of power. Throughout this book I discuss the openness of city space during the industrial era. When American cities functioned as industrial centers, they required a population made up of all economic classes. A successful manufacturing industry required employees ranging from unskilled laborers to white-collar executives. I don't mean to romanticize life during the industrial age. The jobs were often dangerous, and the distribution of wealth was often unfair. American cities became defined as manufacturing centers from the 1870s through the 1920s, witnessed a rash of factory closings during the Great Depression, and saw a revival of factory use for the production of wartime goods from 1939 through 1945. Throughout this, early industrialism in America unfairly distributed wealth to the top 10 percent of wage earners, most of whom worked in high-level industrial jobs. Market income analysis of the years 1917–2005 shows that the top decile of workers earned over 40 percent of the market income for all but three years between 1917 and 1940. In fact, the years 1927 and 1932 saw the top decile earn almost 50 percent of the income that year. City populations exploded during these times, but most of the new residents in Northeastern and Midwestern cities who worked unskilled and semi-skilled jobs were poor European immigrants, while the new population of low-level workers in the Southwest were Mexican immigrants. Thus, while the industrial era saw cities remain open to all social classes, life was often difficult for the economically vulnerable.[7]

The post-World War II era is significant to open spaces for two reasons. First, this is the time of not only television's arrival in American culture, but also of the arrival of what scholars such as Anna McCarthy call "first-wave reality television." These are shows such as Allen Funt's *Candid Camera* (first run, 1948–67) which, while not labelled as reality television during their initial run, have since been reclaimed as reality television for their ability to show real people in real places.[8] Second, the dawn of reality television occurred at a moment of economic egalitarianism in the American industrial economy that affected the openness of space on the genre in several ways. The post-World War II era saw the market income of the top 10 percent of workers drop to 30 percent and saw most of the wealth distributed evenly across the social classes. This was the era of Keynesian economics where an increase in consumer spending, fueled by wartime savings and an ease in credit regulations, increased the demand for employment in manufacturing. Moreover, stronger labor unions negotiated with large corporations for a fair distribution of capital. As a result, various aspects of the American dream—rising in class, owning a home, having a family—became accessible to more citizens than ever before. To accommodate this, and to boost economic prosperity, urban regions expanded to include newly built outer-zone bedroom communities where working-class city dwellers could now purchase middle-class homes. New highways connected these new suburbs to the city, which created even more employment opportunities. Part of America's economic upsurge at this point was due to its position in the world and a global economy. Many European countries incurred significant destruction during World War II and went into a phase of rebuilding in the 1940s and 1950s, a process that not only stunted their economic growth but also required manufactured goods such as steel and heavy machinery. The United States, a country physically undamaged by World War II and still operating in an industrial economy, was able to export crucial resources to these countries. Cities and urban regions were open to all classes, and they were doing better economically than they ever had in the industrial era.[9]

This economic moment shaped the way people conceived of larger spatial relationships. Janet Abu-Lughod argues post-World War II American prosperity created an economic base and social ideology whereby those excluded from the paradise-like economy—African Americans, other racial minorities, women, LGBTQ people—fought to be admitted to this land of equality. The oppression and protests of these social groups predated the postwar era, but the way fair economic prosperity was sold to America emphasized that everyone had a right to happiness and dignity. According to Abu-Lughod, these notions of economic prosperity became inextricably linked to a push for human rights in the period.[10] Certainly they did not generate an awareness of oppression or a core philosophy of resistance, but postwar economic egalitarianism and the push for human rights were part of the same cultural moment that fought for fairness. As a result, we see two layers of openness in postwar urban regions: (1) that they could offer a better life by allowing more people to pursue the American dream, and (2) that they could offer people the opportunity to open oppressive spatial relations involving race, gender, and class in order to fight for better conditions.

During this moment, reality television's precursors, first-wave shows such as *Candid Camera*, *An American Family* (1973), and early seasons of *The Real World*, went into cities open to all economic classes and opened up—by this I mean reworked—oppressive social relationships for utopian and/or liberatory purposes. Chapter One shows how these programs had differing strategies both to depict real life and to open space. Moreover, the shows not only appeared in different decades; they also surfaced on different locations in the universe of channels—network television, public television, and cable television, respectively. Thus, surveying these three shows allows us to understand the macro-level nature of open space on twentieth-century reality television. It also allows us to examine micro-level case studies that show various specificities of open space. *Candid Camera* took part in a postwar television culture that tried to obliterate class hierarchies. Other programs offered highbrow culture typically reserved for the elite to the masses, while *Candid Camera* created an anonymous, generic city where class markers became illegible. In these spaces, the program challenged other spatial relationships such as the personal, emotional, and professional isolation of women in the suburbs. The program humorously opened spaces to women by suggesting that they deserved more than suburban femininity. In 1973, *An American Family* used the film style from the documentary movement Direct Cinema to capture the decay of the patriarchal nuclear family after the radicalism of the 1960s. The program used travel as a form of power geometry to open the family to alternatives to the traditional postwar family lifestyles shaping the spatial relationships in the city of Santa Barbara. Finally, the first season of *The Real World*, which aired in 1992, held onto this twentieth-century spatial egalitarian ethos as it filmed its first season in the gentrifying neighborhood of SoHo in New York. Rather than remain in this elitist space, *The Real World* chose to use the neighborhood as a transportation hub to open up to different, financially impoverished areas of the city.

When I discuss the closed spaces of reality television and global cities in the twenty-first century, I do so not to suggest these spaces are exact opposites to the open spaces of American cities and reality television in the twentieth century. Neither do I mean to suggest that Marxist geographers threw in the towel and gave up resistance when the political economy of social expulsions set in. Massey's *World City*, a brilliant work on the spatial politics of London and its relationship to England when this major metropolis became a global center of finance, details potential sites of resistance and possibilities for opening space in an era where social evictions are commonplace.[11] For example, Massey suggests alternative geographies of allegiance where the downtrodden of London find they have economic problems in common with residents of impoverished post-industrial northern cities such as Manchester and Liverpool. David Harvey's *Rebel Cities: From the Right to the City to Urban Revolution* masterfully examines grassroots resistance to the global transformation of cities by exploring events such as Occupy Wall Street.[12] When I use the term *closed space*, I do so to highlight how residential and leisure access to city spaces is closed off to a majority of people, and reality television adds another layer to closed space by no longer challenging spatial relationships in these urban areas. Reality television, instead, focuses on winning consent for the new closed residencies in cities.

The closed, elitist nature of urban access never could have been foreseen as industrial economies started to die during the 1970s. Cities entered an astonishing state of decline in the 1970s, as manufacturing and industry jobs shut down and were exported to poor countries in the global South so that labor could be done at a significantly lower cost. Unemployment rates skyrocketed in American cities, and poverty intensified. New York City almost declared bankruptcy in 1975 and was saved only by a Municipal Assistance Corporation bond and austerity program typically used by the International Monetary Fund to assist third-world countries.[13] Many cities lost populations, and once-thriving neighborhoods fell into disrepair. It seemed as if great cities were becoming a thing of the past. But the 1980s witnessed key changes in economic policies for cities crucial to a global, post-industrial economy and redefined who could inhabit these spaces.

Sassen argues that cities became important again during the 1980s because of the world economy's need for growing specialized services for firms and finances. The era of global financial services propelled by transnational corporations began, and while new communication technologies allowed for a dispersed business community around the world, global financial networks required centralized places to conduct business. Thus, cities emerged as sites for top-level financial, corporate, and legal service executives to live and work with each other. Cities now function as critical locations for international transactions. Sassen argues that rather than seeing major global cities in America as somehow building a regional workforce or as part of a national economy, we should see them as part of a global financial and business network, making New York, Chicago, Boston, and Los Angeles more tied to the economies of world cities such as London, Tokyo, Paris, and Toronto than to fallen industrial cities such as Buffalo or Detroit. Sassen defines global cities as having three functions: (1) "command points" for the world economy, (2) locations for finance and specialized services, and (3) sites of production for world businesses. In the 1980s, global city economies thrived because of deregulatory polices, often referred to as neoliberal policies, that made wealth accumulation possible for the elite by redirecting it from the poor, working, and middle classes.[14] America's welfare state commitment to combat poverty and its economic policies to help the middle class were cut. As William W. Goldsmith and Edward J. Blake succinctly state, "economic and political forces no longer combat poverty— they generate poverty."[15] Sassen shows how in the 2000s the top 10 percent of workers received 90 percent of the income growth.[16] In fact, in the past 20 years, there has been a 60 percent increase in the total wealth of the top 1 percent. Sassen's most recent scholarship shows how the economy thrives on predatory formations that concentrate wealth within the elite by making life so untenable for a majority of the population in certain areas that expulsions have become a central part of contemporary society.

This has profoundly transformed the populations of global cities, making them home to a group of mobile executives who often move from global city to global city. And while the middle and working classes have been driven out of these spaces through exorbitant costs of living, the areas rely heavily on a servant class that cleans houses, walks dogs, offers laundry services, etc. The result is that America's global cities have been transformed into residential and leisure zones for the elite. Robert Fritch argues that the American global city has become a "kind of high-rise command center" that caters to a wealthy life style.[17]

The spaces of the elites and the servant class are relatively closed off from one another. While the poor are required to enter the spaces of the rich to run their errands and clean their houses, they are not allowed to inhabit the same social spaces outside of work. This came into sharp focus in a recent controversy over "poor doors" being built in Manhattan's new condo buildings. As public housing becomes obsolete, cities now offer substantial tax breaks, subsidies, and incentives for developers to include affordable housing units in luxury high rises. In Manhattan, developers are seizing this money and creating separate entrances so that the rich and the poor who live in the same building will not interact with each other—a form of modern-day segregation that relegates the less fortunate to the margins of the borough to preserve the elitist nature of the area.[18]

Chapters Two through Five of this book offer a series of case studies that use theoretical constructs from the fields of media studies or geography that highlight how reality television assists in winning the consent of its viewers to embrace the political economy of social expulsions. Chapter Two looks at the spectacle of wealth on contemporary urban reality shows by drawing on film theory that has shown that the spectacle and the narrative operate through different political and temporal logics. This helps to illuminate the time-shifting presentation of urban economics on urban reality shows. Spectacular moments divorced from the plot on these shows—montages that transition us from opening credits to scenes, from commercials to scenes, and from scenes to other scenes—are the main ways the shows visualize urban space. These montages present the city at a distance, making the closed spaces of contemporary cities inspire awe and joy. However, the stories told about life in cities and the characters' accents frequently register nostalgia for the industrial organization of society and postwar notions of class mobility. These elements help to win consent for the closed spaces the spectacular montages present, as they are able to convince us that today's cities still operate under industrial logics of class egalitarianism.

Chapter Three examines how Bravo programming is anomalous in the reality television landscape. While reality programs across the channels typically ignore servants, Bravo programs such as The Real Housewives, Vanderpump Rules, and Flipping Out (2007–present) find a variety of ways to bring servants and servers to the screen. The uniqueness of this phenomenon requires a detailed inquiry into the Bravo brand to figure out why servants matter to this channel. Television brands frequently lack coherence, as they are constructed by a group of executives who often have different goals for different sets of programs on the channel. In the 2000s, Bravo reality programming celebrated the affluence of its rich cast members and also ironically laughed at the same cast members for being hypocritical louses, creating a very unstable meaning for these leads. Bravo is able to stabilize the celebratory reading of the elite in its programs by other-ing the servants and servers on the shows. This chapter considers a variety of geographic constructions that redeem the elite as normal and make viewers feel connected more to the elite's privilege than to the servants' and the servers' economic vulnerability.

Chapter Four looks at the way successful reality gamers such as Rob Mariano and Tiffany Pollard built memorable characters by merging urban identities with historical racial and ethnic stereotypes. As the character Boston Rob on CBS's *Survivor* and *The Amazing Race*, Mariano made it to the final two or three contestants on three of the six seasons in which he competed. Pollard played the unforgettable character New York on VH1's *Flavor of Love* (2006–08), *I Love New York* (2007–08), *New York Goes to Hollywood* (2008), and *New York Goes to Work* (2009). There are three commonalities that Mariano and Pollard share: (1) they each represent a city, (2) they each represent that city in spaces that are not those cities, and (3) they each perform historically grounded, offensive stereotypes of their ethnic or racial group. Mariano plays the roles of the Italian American gangster and trickster that have roots in the first wave of Italian immigration in the early twentieth century. New York plays the black sapphire, the loud and aggressive black woman cre-ated in the white imagination to provoke intra-racial conflict among African Americans after the slaves were freed. Boston Rob and New York represent very different views on the place of their social group within contemporary American urban cultures. White working-class neighborhoods are increas-ingly disappearing in the era of social expulsions. Rob's popularity as a CBS reality persona speaks to a nostalgic vision in urban life, and his success in the game makes residual urban identities seem more prominent than they are in today's cities. New York's stereotypical identity registers historical continuity. New York was a key figure in VH1 growing its own celebrities instead of resurrecting figures from popular culture's past. New York helped focus VH1 programming more on the now than on the past, and her suc-cess speaks to how the poor African American is a figure from the past who still occupies today's global cities. A comparative study of these two reveals how reality television has to win our consent for the political economy of expulsions by imagining how expelled Italian American identities are still central to contemporary cities. But the persistence of black poverty in global cities means VH1 does not have to time shift African American identities to make them seem relevant to contemporary urbanity.

Chapter Five concludes the book with a look at how the subgenre of rural reality programs wins consent for the contemporary political economy of social expulsions. As Raymond Williams argues, the country and the city have a symbiotic relationship in fiction. The country often serves as an imagined space that offers desired qualities that we find lacking in cities.[19] Thus, I investigate rural reality programs to see how they both offer a temporary escape from and a reaffirmation of values of contemporary urbanity. A group of programs that includes Swamp People (2010–present), Moonshiners (2011–present), Alaska: The Last Frontier (2011–present), and Buying Alaska (2012–15) nostalgically portray the country as a pre-modern space untainted by the problems of the political economy of social expulsions. This offers an unrealistic view of the country as a place untouched by expulsions (when, in fact, rural spaces are subject to their own types of expulsions), and it posits many qualities in the country (the ability to live life in one place and the ability to work one job, for example) that many people found in post-World War II industrial cities. Other reality programs such as Here Comes Honey Boo Boo (2012–14) use an urban viewing lens to look at the country with derision. The country becomes a place of disgust, of backward practices, that makes us embrace the values of contemporary cities.

These five chapters come together to show the macro-level change of the open spaces of twentieth-century reality television becoming the closed spaces of twenty-first-century reality television. Whereas reality television once went into spaces open to all classes in the industrial era to rework oppressive spatial relationships for liberatory purposes, reality television now tries to win our consent for the closed spaces of the twenty-first-century political economy of expulsions.

THE DEFINITION OF REALITY TELEVISION

Most people have an immediate reaction to the mention of reality television—they react with appreciation or disgust. Reality television is such a ubiquitous part of today's television culture that even people who don't watch it have a basic understanding of what it is. In fact, a common understanding of the genre's premises makes it possible for me to be near the end of this introduction without having defined the genre. However, it is worth specifying how I frame the genre, if only to set up clear limits on the types of reality programs that concern me in this study. This book is not an encyclopedic history of all reality television subgenres; neither is it a precise history of the term, tracing exactly when it surfaces in television history and how the term is projected on the past to reclaim certain programs as the first wave of the genre. Rather, taking my lead from historian Keith Jenkins, my history of reality television is based on his concept of history. History is a combination of the past (all that has happened before the present) and historiography (the writing of history, which privileges interpretation and foregrounding some material while ignoring others).[20] Analyzing reality television's engagement with twentieth- and twenty-first-century spatial politics requires focusing on a certain type of reality program (and ignoring others that are not interested in the presentation of urbanity).

For this book, I define reality television as programs that show real people (not trained and/or unionized actors) in real locations (not a television studio) functioning in situations that resemble their real lives or in situations that were constructed by television producers. This definition allows us to investigate televisual portraits of the real geographic locations in various types of reality subgenres such as gamedocs, real-estate programming, and docu-soaps. Some people might be surprised that a book on reality television would group real-estate programs with reality game shows, but this book will show how these programs are linked by a similar conception of space. Other people might wonder why popular programs such as *Dancing with the Stars* (2005–present) and *The Voice* (2011–present) are absent from this book. My definition of reality television purposefully ignores contemporary reality programs and precursors to the genre that were shot entirely or mostly in studio spaces. For example, scholars such as Kevin Glynn masterfully argue that reality television and studio-shot talk shows both belong to the category of tabloid television, which prioritizes scandal, gossip, and people marginalized from mainstream society.[21] Other media scholars such as Henry Jenkins have examined studio-based reality talent competitions such as *American Idol*, which involve audience members voting via phone or the internet for winners, and Amber Watts writes convincingly about the 1950s studio series *Queen for a Day* (1956–64), a first-wave reality show that used a studio audience to vote on which real person on stage had the worst life.[22] My history of reality television ignores studio-based reality television in order to examine the way a majority of programming within the genre represents the complex dynamics of real social spaces. Including studio-based reality television distorts the focus of this theme in the genre.

To construct a history of reality television that moves from the twentieth to the twenty-first century, I continue a trend in reality television scholarship that looks at the so-called first-wave programs such as *Candid Camera*, *An American Family*, and *The Real World*. None of these shows were referred to as reality television when first released. Rather, academics, journalists, and industry workers have used a variety of terms to reclaim these shows as reality television, such as calling them the "parents" or "grandparents" of reality television. Occasionally a scholar or journalist will claim one of these shows is "the first reality television show" or "the original reality television show."

The fact that these programs were classified through other genres when they were initially released does not disqualify them from historical analysis as reality television programs. Generic classification is a complex process. Media studies scholars such as James Naremore, Rick Altman, and Jason Mittell argue that genres exist as discursive fields, not as stable sets of texts with permanent textual features and not as biological entities that evolve on a predetermined path over time.[23] As Altman writes, "Genres are not inert categories shared by all (though at some moments they certainly seem to be), but discursive claims made by real speakers for particular purposes in specific situations."[24] In his brilliant study of film noir, Naremore argues that the category did not exist when the films were initially made in the 1940s and that film noir is both an idea that intellectuals and popular culture have projected onto the past and an important cinematic legacy. Naremore shows how French intellectuals created the category in the 1950s. Naremore, though, still finds value in looking at textual features of genre such as cinematography, lighting, etc., after he explains that film noir was discursively created after these films were made. My study of reality television is indebted to the work of each of these groundbreaking genre theorists, but especially to Naremore, as I look at textual features of programs reclaimed as reality television.

I acknowledge that we have projected the category of reality television onto texts of the twentieth century such as *Candid Camera*, *An American Family*, and *The Real World*. My goal is not to unearth the original generic classifications of these shows and then show the complex process by which they have been reclaimed as reality television, although that would make for a fascinating research project. Neither do I claim that these are the only twentieth-century texts that have been recast as reality television. Rather, I use these texts to map out a larger history that involves a major shift between the open spaces of twentieth-century reality programs and the closed spaces of twenty-first-century reality programs.

I should point out something rather obvious; nevertheless, it is something that needs to be said. Reality television isn't "real." I always love it when someone finds out that I write about reality television and then asks me, "You know reality television isn't real, right?" The individual usually follows with an intense stare that suggests the revelation will cause me to melt away like I'm the Wicked Witch of the West at the end of *The Wizard of Oz* (1939). Although the reality television programs I analyze show real people in real locations, they mediate reality through narrative practices; aesthetic choices; geographic constructs; thematic interests; casting decisions; and social, economic, political, and cultural power. As should be clear from the argument of this book, reality television is not locating a reality about city life and conveying it to viewers. Rather, it is constructing a reality that makes it seem like American global cities serve our interests. Each chapter pays special attention to certain aspects of the mediation of city life on reality television.

THE FOCUS ON AMERICAN REALITY TELEVISION

Why does this project focus exclusively on American reality television? With a focus on the political economy of social expulsions that arose when American cities became global cities, it's a question worth asking. Indeed, reality television is a genre that spans across the globe. Recent anthologies such as Brenda Weber's *Reality Gendervision: Sexuality and Gender on Transatlantic*

Television and Marwan M. Kraidy and Katherine Sender's *The Politics of Reality Television: Global Perspectives* make a convincing case for studying reality television in a global context.[25] Weber productively shows how Britain and the United States frequently share reality programs. *The Apprentice* (2004–present), *America's Next Top Model* (2003–present), and *The Biggest Loser* (2004–present) began in the United States and were then remade in England. Likewise, Britain's *Pop Idol* (2001–03) was adapted as *American Idol* (2002–16). Weber finds an incestuous relationship between America and Britain and its reality television, pinpointing ways that the nations' reality programs are tied together through production and distribution.[26] Likewise, Sender sees the globalization of reality television as marked by the global flow of formulas appropriated within distinct national and local settings.[27]

Despite the global reach of the urban economy and reality television, examining the national inflection of both reality television and the political economies of social expulsions can produce compelling findings. Sender argues "neoliberalism is not an undifferentiated global phenomenon but is articulated differently in regional and national contexts."[28] For the sake of this project, the economic conditions that preceded neoliberalism in the United States were distinct. American economic prosperity surfaced in part because so much of the rest of the globe was rebuilding after World War II and reliant on American manufacturing and industry, a phenomenon that made America's economy grow much faster than the economies of other nations. Given Abu-Lughod's argument that human rights were tied to economic equality in postwar America, we can see a unique national inflection of open space appearing on twentieth-century reality television. Additionally, the surge in the postwar American economy spoke to national conceptions of the American dream and the right to class mobility.

The economic policies in America that proceeded from a global deregulated economy were exceptional as well. Sociologists have shown that the United States has reduced its welfare state more than other advanced countries have. Abu-Lughod argues that among Sweden, the United Kingdom, Australia, Canada, and Germany, the United States' welfare system "lagged considerably behind the other developed nations."[29] Thus, there is a unique American perspective of individual neoliberal advancement that ignores the plight of the poor and marginalized more intensely than other national perspectives. Moreover, regressive taxes within the United States tax the middle class and poor heavily while offering huge tax cuts to the top 1 percent of wage earners. That, coupled with the weakening of labor unions and the movement from fulltime employees to independent contracting, has led to a more intense class polarization than is found in other developed countries.

All of this comes together to make the way American reality television tries to win the consent for the political economy of social expulsions exceptional. The economic prosperity in America before the 1980s offered an unprecedented fair distribution of wealth between the classes, and the brutality of America's inflection of social expulsions is harsher than it is in other countries.

WHAT WE CAN ACCOMPLISH BY TELLING THE HISTORY OF REALITY TELEVISION FROM THE PERSPECTIVE OF URBAN SPACE

As a media scholar, one of my commitments is to investigate the relationship between media and culture with a special eye on social oppression so that my writing may help to imagine a more just future. With this specific book, I acknowledge that developing a critical media literacy about reality television's ability to win consent for urban social expulsions will not in and of itself arrest this political inequality. But developing this literacy is an important step to creating equality-minded social change where, rather than accepting a television genre's arguments that cities serve our interests, we realize the injustices of the system and the complex ways that television makes them seem just.

When we narrate the history of American reality television from the perspective of city locations, we see that the closed nature of space on urban reality television shows and the way those programs try to win our consent does not have to be. As Massey claims, spatial relationships are never set. They are always open to reinterpretation. The first-wave shows of the twentieth century that I examine represent one such way that reality programs can open space. One of the goals of this book, then, is to show the way spatial relationships used to operate on reality television so that we can begin to reimagine the way space could function on twenty-first-century reality television. Whether media students go on to work on reality television shows after graduating from college or whether they continue to watch reality television throughout their lives, students of reality television can use this history to think about ways that reality programs can open the spatial relationships of America's global cities and other spaces as well.

NOTES

1 Reality television scholars view the genre through these eight critical lenses: (1) neoliberalism (i.e., the way reality television offers the tools for citizens to avert risks, to claim personal responsibility, and not to rely on the government for assistance); (2) advertisement (i.e., the way reality television increasingly incorporates elements of public relations and advertisement); (3) interactivity (i.e., to what extent reality television allows for audience participation more than other genres do and then to what extent that renders the genre democratic or corporately controlled); (4) realism (i.e., to what extent can the contrived situations in reality television make it compatible with a realist aesthetic and to what extent the filming of ordinary people on reality television is indebted to documentary traditions); (5) voyeurism (i.e., the way the aesthetics and technologies on the show position audience members as voyeurs); (6) ordinariness (i.e., the way ordinary people are featured and made into stars in the genre); (7) globalism (the way reality television formats circulate around the world and are appropriate for specific national and local contexts); and (8) various ways to theorize gender, race, and class.

The key monographs that offer an introduction to the history of reality television are June Deery, *Reality TV* (London: Polity Press, 2015); Misha Kavka, *Reality TV* (Edinburgh, UK: Edinburgh University Press, 2012); and Leigh H. Edwards, *The Triumph of Reality TV: The Revolution of American Television* (New York: Praeger, 2012).

The edited anthologies that survey approaches to reality television are David S. Escoffery, ed., *How Real is Reality TV?: Essays on Representation and Truth* (Jefferson, NC: McFarland Press, 2006); Su Homes and Deborah Jermyn, eds, *Understanding Reality Television* (New York: Routledge, 2004); Susan Murray and Laurie Ouellette, eds, *Reality TV: Remaking Television Culture* (New York: New York University Press, 2004, 2009); and Laurie Ouellette, ed., *A Companion to Reality TV* (Malden, MA: Wiley-Blackwell, 2013).

The specialized monographs and anthologies that present a focused argument on an aspect of reality television are Mark Andrejevic, *Reality TV: The Work of Being Watched* (Boulder, CO: Rowman and Littlefield, 2003); Jonathan Bignell, *Big Brother: Reality TV in the Twenty-First Century* (New York: Palgrave Macmillan, 2005); Anita Biressi and Heather Nunn, *Reality TV: Realism and Revelation* (London: Wallflower Press, 2005); June Deery, *Consuming Reality: The Commercialization of Factual Entertainment* (New York: Palgrave Macmillan, 2012); Jon Dovey, *Freakshow: First Person Media and Factual Television* (London: Pluto Press, 2000); Rachel E. Dubrofsky, *The Surveillance of Women on Reality Television: Watching the Bachelor and the Bachelorette* (Lanham, MD: Lexingiton, 2011); Dana Heller, ed., *Makeover Television: Realities Remodeled* (London: I.B. Taurus, 2007); Annette Hill, *Reality TV: Factual Entertainment and Television Audiences* (New York: Routledge, 2005); Annette Hill, *Restyling Factual Television: Audiences and News, Documentary, and Reality Genres* (New York: Routledge, 2007); Misha Kavka, *Reality Television, Affect, and Intimacy: Reality Matters* (New York: Palgrave Macmillan, 2008); Laurie Ouellette and James Hay, *Better Living Through Reality TV: Television and Post-Welfare Citizenship* (Malden, MA: Wiley-Blackwell, 2008); Gareth Palmer, ed., *Exposing Lifestyle Television* (London: Ashgate, 2008); Katherine Sender, *The Makeover: Reality TV and the Reflexive Audience* (New York: New York University Press, 2012); Marwan Kraidy and Katherine Sender, eds, *The Politics of Reality Television: Global Perspectives* (New York: Routledge, 2011); Jervette R. Ward, ed., *Real Sister: Stereotypes, Respectability, and Black Women in Reality TV* (New Brunswick, NJ: Rutgers University Press, 2015); Brenda Weber, *Makeover TV: Selfhood, Citizenship, and Celebrity* (Durham, NC: Duke University Press, 2009); and Brenda Weber, ed., *Reality Gendervision: Sexuality & Gender on Transatlantic Reality Television* (Durham, NC: Duke University Press, 2014).

2 Saskia Sassen, *Expulsions: Brutality and Complexity in the Global Economy* (Cambridge, MA: Harvard University Press, 2014), 1.

3 Kevin Lynch, *The Image of the City* (Cambridge, MA: The MIT Press, 1960), 9.

4 Frederic Jameson, *The Geopolitical Aesthetic: Cinema and Space in the World System* (Bloomington, IN: Indiana University Press, 1992).

5 Henri Lefebvre, *The Production of Space*, trans. Donald Nicholson-Smith (Malden, MA: Blackwell Publishing, 1991), 10–11.

6. Raymond Williams, *Marxism and Literature* (New York: Oxford University Press, 1978), 121–7.

7 Janet L. Abu-Lughod, *New York, Chicago, Los Angeles: America's Global Cities* (Minneapolis, MN: University of Minnesota Press, 1999).

8 Anna McCarthy, "Stanley Milgram, Allen Funt, and Me: Postwar Social Science and the 'First Wave' of Reality TV," in Susan Murray and Laurie Ouellette, eds, *Reality TV: Remaking Television Culture*, 1st edition (New York: New York University Press, 2004), 19–39.

9 Janet L. Abu-Lughod, *New York, Chicago, Los Angeles: America's Global Cities* (Minneapolis, MN: University of Minnesota Press, 1999), 173–5; Saskia Sassen, *Expulsions: Brutality and Complexity in the Global Economy* (Cambridge, MA: Harvard University Press, 2014), 17.

10 Janet L. Abu-Lughod, *New York, Chicago, Los Angeles: America's Global Cities* (Minneapolis, MN: University of Minnesota Press, 1999), 173.

11 Doreen Massey, *World City* (London: Polity, 2007).

12 David Harvey, *Rebel Cities: From the Right to the City to the Urban Revolution* (New York: Verso, 2012).

13 Janet L. Abu-Lughod, *New York, Chicago, Los Angeles: America's Global Cities* (Minneapolis, MN: University of Minnesota Press, 1999), 283.

14 Saskia Sassen, *Cities in a World Economy*, 4th edition (London: Sage, 2012), 1–115.

15 William G. Goldsmith and Edward J. Blakely, *Separate Societies: Poverty and Inequality in U.S. Cities* (Philadelphia, PA: Temple University Press, 1992), 1.

16 Saskia Sassen, *Expulsions: Brutality and Complexity in the Global Economy* (Cambridge, MA: Harvard University Press, 2014), 14.

17 Robert Fritch, *The Assignation of New York* (London: Verso, 1993), 235–7.

18 Mireya Navarro, "'Poor Door' in a New York Tower Opens a Fight over Affordable Housing." *The New York Times*. August 26, 2014. Accessed September 25, 2014. http://www.nytimes.com/2014/08/27/nyregion/separate-entryways-for-new-york-condo-buyers-and-renters-create-an-affordable-housing-dilemma.html?_r=0.

19 Raymond Williams, *The Country and the City* (New York: Oxford University Press, 1973), 17.

20 Keith Jenkins, *Re-Thinking History* (New York: Routledge, 1991).

21 Kevin Glynn, *Tabloid Culture: Trash Taste, Popular Power, and the Transformation of American Television* (Durham, NC: Duke University Press, 2000).

22 Henry Jenkins, *Convergence Culture: Where Old and New Media Collide* (New York: New York University Press, 2007), 59–92; Amber Watts, "Melancholy, Merit, and Merchandise: The Postwar Audience Participation Show," in Susan Murray and Laurie Ouellette, eds, *Reality TV: Remaking Television Culture*, 2nd edition (New York: New York University Press, 2004), 301–20.

23 Rick Altman, *Film/Genre* (London: British Film Institute, 1999); James Naremore, *More Than Night: Film Noir in its Contexts* (Berkeley, CA: University of California Press, 1998); Jason Mittell, *Genre and Television: From Cop Shows to Cartoons in American Culture* (New York: Routledge, 2004).

24 Rick Altman, *Film/Genre* (London: British Film Institute, 1999), 101.

25 Brenda Weber, ed., *Reality Gendervision: Sexuality & Gender on Transatlantic Reality Television* (Durham, NC: Duke University Press, 2014); Marwan Kraidy and Katherine Sender, eds, *The Politics of Reality Television: Global Perspectives* (New York: Routledge, 2011).

26 Brenda Weber, "Introduction: Trash Talk: Gender as an Analytic on Reality Television," in Brenda Weber, ed. *Reality Gendervision: Sexuality & Gender on Transatlantic Reality Television* (Durham, NC: Duke University Press, 2014), 6–8.

27 Katherine Sender, "Real Worlds: Migrating Genres, Travelling Participants, Shifting Theories," in Marwan Kraidy and Katherine Sender, eds, *The Politics of Reality Television: Global Perspectives* (New York: Routledge, 2011), 1.

28 Katherine Sender, "Real Worlds: Migrating Genres, Travelling Participants, Shifting Theories," in Marwan Kraidy and Katherine Sender, eds, *The Politics of Reality Television: Global Perspectives* (New York: Routledge, 2011), 5.

29 Janet L. Abu-Lughod, *New York, Chicago, Los Angeles: America's Global Cities* (Minneapolis, MN: University of Minnesota Press, 1999), 278.

1

THE OPENNESS OF SPACE
ON TWENTIETH-CENTURY
REALITY TELEVISION

Reality television's precursors appeared sporadically on television schedules in the twentieth century. *Candid Camera* (first run, 1948–67) went through a series of cancellations and reappearances from 1948–92. The show shifted on the schedules in the 1950s, airing for three years in syndication and then reappearing on NBC in 1958 as a segment on *The Jack Paar Tonight Show* (1957–62) and on CBS in 1959 as part of *The Garry Moore Show* (1950–67). *Candid Camera*'s longest consecutive run was on CBS as a Sunday evening show from 1960–67. *An American Family* became a sensation in 1973 but failed to generate any cycle of reality television in the 1970s, and *The Real World* (1992–present) premiered on MTV in 1992. These programs appeared at different historical moments and surfaced in different locations on television, ranging from broadcast to public to cable television. Although these programs have been reclaimed as reality television's grandparents and parents, or the "first wave" of reality television, they differ from each other in their strategies for entering real spaces and their depictions of ordinary people.

The few examples of reality shows from the twentieth century appeared in different historical climates, which had an interesting effect on the open nature of space on these programs. At a macro-level, these programs open space by going into egalitarian spaces associated with the industrial organization of society to show areas inhabited by all classes and by portraying social relations in these spaces as malleable in order to liberate people from oppression. But from a micro-level, these shows—because they are so spread out in the history of twentieth-century television—are marked by three significant differences: (1) they engage with very different, historically situated constructions of televisual realism and notions of the ordinary; (2) they interact with contrasting discourses of reality associated with early broadcast, public, and cable television; and (3) they engage with different social issues shaping the experience of space in their contemporary culture. These three items influence the way space is presented aesthetically, politically, and culturally on each program. This chapter looks at how the historical poetics of these programs interact with larger social issues to open urban space.

TURNING ORDINARY PLACES INTO EXTRAORDINARY SPACES ON *CANDID CAMERA*

Space is a defining feature of *Candid Camera*. Each episode involves show creator Allen Funt and a cohost—and sometimes the prank actors—introducing the sketches to a studio audience. Sketches were shot in real locales, typically in the New York City area—either inside a business, on city streets, or on highways. But *Candid Camera* travelled the United States and the world, shooting in Arizona, London, Paris, and Moscow. *Candid Camera* went to urban locations open to all classes and re-opened the social relationships structuring those spaces. *Candid Camera* filtered these spatial politics through discourses of the ordinary and the extraordinary in an effort to capture how life is lived and how life could be lived. The show was part of a post-World War II television cultural moment that embraced the medium for its ability to convey realism, but *Candid Camera* challenged what realism was and how real life could operate.

Space on *Candid Camera* is simultaneously specific and generic. This tension develops through the show's dual format. Studio segments have Funt, his cohost, and the actors introduce each sketch through an explanation of where filming takes place—right down to a specific address, a specific store, or a specific highway. The studio segments create a detailed linguistic map with exact coordinates for each prank. The mapping process operates through what Kent C. Ryden calls a cartographic discourse, which:

> replaces geography with geometry, meaning with measurement. The geodetic viewpoint sees the earth not as a collection of spaces to be experienced but as a surface to be measured. . . . It just looks from survey marker to survey marker, thinks about where one mathematical point is in relation to another mathematical point.[1]

The emphasis on precise locations never ventures into a discussion of local cultures.

The on-location shooting used an aesthetic that made space generic. In "The Talking Mailbox" sketch, Funt places a microphone in a New York City mailbox. A crew sits in a car several feet away. One crew member talks

Figure 1.1 Allen Funt and Bess Meyerson during a studio segment of *Candid Camera*.

to people who pass the mailbox. Another crew member secretly films these encounters through a car window. The covert nature of filming never visually maps space in complete ways. Funt used long shots to capture the prank in action. Initially he had his camera operator switch the lenses for a close up of the victim's reaction. Eventually a zoom replaced the lens switch.[2] "The Talking Mailbox" begins with a long shot of the mailbox. The foreground of the frame includes a New York City mailbox. The middle third is a street intersection. The remaining third shows a city block. A drug store is across the street, but the framing fails to include the store's name, though it does show the attached buildings. The image lacks visual clarity; it doesn't show if the attached buildings have stores on the bottom level or if they are strictly apartment buildings. The visual information is so generic that this could be any street corner in a U.S. city. Funt switches to a medium shot and then a close up as he continues with each person who approaches the mailbox. The medium shot provides some information about the locale, but it is even less specific. We can now see words such as "air mail" and "delivery" on the mailbox, but we now see just the side of the drug store, which reveals in more detail a window display on cold remedies. The close up includes just the victim's face and torso and the mail box to reveal the participant's shock.

Funt preferred indoor shoots because of the technical difficulties of shooting outside; indoor shoots also portray space generically. Funt felt the ambient noise of outside shoots overpowered the sound of filmed participants. Inside shoots allowed for precise placement of hidden mics. Additionally, Funt used two-way mirrors inside to conceal the camera. Funt also believed that lighting presented a problem outside, as natural light often made the image too dark.[3] One such indoor location Funt chose was Bickford's Diner in Queens for the "Amplified Eating Sounds" sketch. They placed mics above and below a counter to magnify the sound of a person eating by thirty times. The camera was set up behind a two-way mirror in the kitchen. Although a few shots include a Bickford's menu, there is no larger construction of neighborhood space. No exteriors display the neighborhood. The interior long shots are so generic that this could be any diner in the United States. The sketch goes between the long shot establishing the space of the diner to close ups of people's comically disturbed reactions to the magnified sound. The specifics of space are told to the studio and television audience, but these specifics are not captured visually on screen.

Space is never exclusionary on *Candid Camera*. The generic depictions of urban locales make it seem like these spaces are open to any citizen. Funt was very fond of "The Talking Mailbox" skit because many of the people who talked to the mailbox were working class, but he loved that an uptight wealthy man talked to the mailbox just like everyone else.[4] The generic depictions of space make it impossible to know the class dynamics of neighborhoods shown on screen. For instance, the sketch "Door on a Vacant Lot" purposefully contrasts class codes. In the studio segment, Funt tells the audience they filmed on an abandoned lot on the East Side. He then tells the audience they put a door frame with the address 440 East 84th Street in the middle of the lot and had a package delivered there. The long shot of the lot shows land littered with crushed concrete. The joke is that the voice that answers the delivery man's ring is a man with a refined British accent. The joke becomes funnier when the Brit asks the delivery man to come through the door and wait for him at the table in the middle of the lot. After the delivery man enters, the Brit comes in and proceeds to have a cup of tea. The class codes cancel each other out in a story about a city that anyone can inhabit; however, those familiar with the address 440 East 84th would know this is in the exclusive part of the Upper East Side near the mayor's house, Gracie Mansion. Despite this, the anonymity of space on *Candid Camera* has an egalitarian ethos.

The indecipherability of classed locations on *Candid Camera* resonated with a larger sense of spatial reorganization brought about by television in the postwar era. Postwar television industry workers spoke about the medium's ability to construct spatial relationships that obliterated cultural hierarchies created through class stratification. Western culture placed the arts in a common culture until the nineteenth century, when society divided tastes along class lines and made the arts occupy geographic zones reserved for the upper class. Plays went from being attended by all classes to being priced for the elite. Literature moved from common culture to universities reserved for the elite. Museums opened up in wealthy areas of towns.[5] Although these class-based taste cultures continued to thrive in the twentieth century, television challenged them in order to create virtual space where all classes could share the same culture. In the late 1940s, a majority of television was shot live in New York City. Broadcasting technology allowed a live performance in New York City to be distributed live to remote areas of the country so that culture was no longer reserved for the urban elite. Armina Marshall, a member of the Theatre Guild—a Broadway production company also active in radio and television—said their broadcast programs "were designed to bring living theatre into the homes of millions . . . especially in those areas where professionally mounted stage plays were not available to the public."[6] Elsewhere, I have argued that some 1950s television dramas became associated with postwar art cinema, but whereas art films only showed in a select number of elite film theatres in cities and college towns, television dramas brought this sophisticated form of narrative to the mass audience.[7]

Funt's urban landscapes maintained a virtual space that levelled classed distinctions. Although post-World War II industrial society required all classes to live in cities, urban areas still had neighborhoods that housed a specific class population. Rich areas of cities such as New York's Upper East Side were still unaffordable to middle and working classes, who would more than likely live in the outer boroughs. Funt's program is unique in that, while other programs sought to level class from the standpoint of a text's cultural heritage, Funt levelled class by making all urban areas part of the same generic classless space.

Funt's commitment to this politics of space stemmed from his own contradictory relationship to class structures. Funt's class status is complicated due to his father's financial successes and failures as a businessman. Sometimes the family had enough money to vacation in Europe, and at others times they could not pay bills. However, Funt's family was well off enough to send Allen and his sister to the elite Ivy League university Cornell. Funt earned riches in the radio and television industry that allowed him to own an Upper East Side townhome.[8] Still, Funt downplayed his connection to wealth and often spoke of his life in terms of its working-class roots. In his autobiography, Funt writes, "I was born in Brooklyn, New York, on September 16, 1914. My early days were spent in an apartment on Flatbush Avenue in a modest neighborhood of immigrants and working-class people."[9] Funt believed that his upbringing as a member of the working class gave him an everyman persona that allowed him to assume any role and remain in disguise.

Funt believed working-class identities were real, authentic, and ordinary; his early efforts in nonfiction television to capture reality were shaped by postwar conceptions of sincerity and deception stemming from an industrial society. Anti-corporate books of the 1950s, such as C. Wright Mills' *White Collar: The American Middle Classes*, David Riesman's *The Lonely Crowd*, and William H. Whyte, Jr.'s, *The Organization Man*, portrayed mid-level white-collar workers as losing their personal identities to follow company mandates. Popular 1950s books such as John Keats' *The Crack in the Picture Window* suggested that the middle classes were so taken by postwar consumer culture and lifestyles that people abandoned critical aspects of humanity.[10]

However, postwar society frequently associated authenticity and realness with the working class because their salt-of-the earth mentality protected them from the insincere traps of middle-class life. For example, postwar television drama often focused on working-class characters to depict realness. In the 1950s, television dramatist Paddy Chayefsky said, "I write about the people I understand—the $75 to $175 a week people."[11] Chayefsky's commitment to displaying ordinary, working-class folks in his television dramas appeared in his famous statement about the difference between film, theatre, and television. He claimed that film presents extraordinary people in extraordinary events, theatre places ordinary people in extraordinary circumstances, and television captures ordinary people in ordinary events.[12] This statement aligned television drama with sincerity because the working-class characters could be who they are in real life, because they experience no artifice.

When Funt claimed the goal of his show was to catch people in the act of being themselves, he was activating a larger discourse about which classes have access to natural, ordinary selves and which classes have been removed from their real selves through consumer culture and class customs.[13] Funt repeats throughout his autobiography that blue-collar people had an easier time "being themselves" in *Candid Camera* pranks.

A look at Funt's commitment to the extraordinary reveals how he further opened space on his programs by reworking social relationships. Funt's original concept was for a radio show titled *Candid Microphone* (1947–48), which would record ordinary life. (*Candid Microphone* became *Candid Camera*.) After many boring skits, Funt realized he needed a provocateur—someone who could introduce extraordinary events into ordinary life.[14] The idea of the provocateur might seem like a juvenile concept, but when Funt noted the figure helped him "rewrite the script of everyday living to test people's responses," he explained how his program re-imagined how people construct their social relationships within space.[15] Funt used the notion of script as a written text to suggest society and its institutions author our lives. Customs are determined by others, not us. The term *script* also resonated within medical discourses where a prescription is "something that is suggested as a way to do something or make something happen."[16] The use of the term *script* in a medical sense became popular in the 1950s. Funt envisioned the provocateur as altering the way suggested social relationships work.

Funt claims *Candid Camera*'s provocations place "the average man in a small crisis," a phrase indebted to postwar leftist theatre and its quest to create a more humane society. Funt's wording is similar to Arthur Miller's famous phrase "tragedy of the common man." Miller announced his theory in a February 27, 1949 article in *The New York Times*, three years before Funt theorized the average man in a small crisis in his book *Eavesdropper at Large*. Miller's essay is most remembered for ripping away the tragic condition from the aristocracy to claim that people of even the lower classes could experience tragedy. More important here is how tragedy teaches and where tragedy is located. Miller claims, "The tragic feeling is evoked in us when we are in the presence of a character who is ready to lay down his life, if need be, to be secure in one thing—his sense of personal dignity."[17] This sentence places a sense of tragedy within the audience, not the character on the stage. The lead character strives for a happiness denied and is destroyed because society will not accommodate such a position. But the audience's perception of these tragic events leads to its enlightenment. Miller writes, "Tragedy enlightens—as it must, in that it points the heroic finger at the enemy of man's freedom. The thrust for freedom is the quality in tragedy which exalts. The revolutionary questioning of the stable environment is what terrifies."[18] While the tragic hero is destroyed through the plot of a play, the audience learns lessons on how to change society to afford more people dignity.

Similarly, Funt's average man in a small crisis did not change the awareness of the unsuspecting person in the skit; it enlightened the audience about an oppressive social structure that permeates spaces of economic equality in the postwar era. Funt was amazed that people would remain unphased by provocateurs and carry on as if things were normal. Funt placed a narrative emphasis on the reveal, the moment where the provocateur informed the person that he or she was on *Candid Camera*. Funt determined that people usually reacted by laughing, by failing to recognize the situation was a joke, or by leaving. Throughout the skit and the reveal, the audience revels in uncontrollable laughter, a response that aligns them with alternative ways of organizing spatial relationships.

One example of this in practice occurs through the provocateur's extraordinary challenge to spatial politics in skits about postwar femininity. The oppression of women in the 1950s registered partly through their spatial isolation. The expansion of urban regions to outer-commuter zones meant that many working-class women who rose to the middle class did so with an accompanying move to remote suburbs. Women who experienced spatial and professional mobility during World War II, working in jobs left open when men went to war, and socializing with extended family and long-time friends in the city, now were stay-at-home mothers in geographically removed neighborhoods. This isolation affected the mental health of many suburban women. Harold Sampson, Sheldon Messinger, and Robert Towne argue that women faced mental stress at the time because of "the increasing isolation of the wife from family and social relationships [and] her more-or-less progressive detachment from participation in social reality."[19] Carol Warren argues that postwar suburban women encountered "loneliness, isolation, and the stress of the housewife role."[20]

Candid Camera included many skits that opened space for women by freeing them from their geographic immobility in the suburbs. In "Allen Rides in a Trunk," Dorothy Collins plays a suburban housewife who locks her husband, Funt, in the trunk of the car after an argument. Collins then drives to New York City. The skit reworks concepts of entrapment, freedom, and gender associated with the postwar suburban movement. The woman holds the mobile position within this marriage, and the man remains literally trapped. This skit at first pretends that this extraordinary occurrence is completely ordinary. As the gas station attendant fills the tank, Collins talks to Funt in the trunk. Collins and Funt ask each other typical questions, such as how much money did the gas cost and should they lunch before arriving in the city. The skit progresses to attacking the foundations of suburban marriage. Funt initially earns the attendant's sympathies, telling him his wife locked him in the trunk after a fight and won't let him out because he has a violent temper. He pleads with the attendant to let him out and asks if he sounds violent. After Funt charms the guy, Funt, enraged, asks, "Well then what are you waiting for? Let me out!" causing the attendant to retreat to his office in fear. Collins then hits the road with Funt still locked in the trunk while the studio audience laughs. Here the laughter stems from repressed feelings that patriarchal culture enacts a form of violence against women by blocking them from their previous social and professional mobility during the war years. The laughter at the sketch's punchline aligns the audience with Collins' quest to escape.

Female pranksters became associated with cars on *Candid Camera*; skits frequently attack notions of the stereotypical female driver. Virginia Scharff argues that this stereotype—that women are accident prone, traffic law violators, and ignorant of auto mechanics—surfaced over fears about "what women might do with plenty of money, big powerful machines, and relatively unrestricted freedom of movement."[21] *Candid Camera*'s ditsy female drivers played into these fears used to justify women's isolation in the suburbs. For the "Splitting Car" sketch, Funt worked with a team of engineers to create a station wagon that would split in half while someone was driving it; another set of wheels were behind the front seat. When Dorothy L'Amour hit a button, the rear half of the car would detach and the front end would keep going. L'Amour brilliantly plays the ditz as she lures men to drive with her, asking if they can figure out what is wrong with her car. She drives approximately twenty feet and then splits the car. When the men scream that her car just broke in half, L'Amour plays dumb, saying she thinks she hears something wrong but isn't sure what happened. The laughter comes from the fact that these men who appear to know more about cars than L'Amour are making comments so obvious that they seem like fools. The woman playing the fool knows more about the situation than any of the men who try to help.

The "Car Without a Motor" skit is even more powerful with its critique of the figure of the ditsy female driver. Funt removed the motor from a convertible, and then has a tow truck push the car down a hill into a gas station with Dorothy Collins driving the car. Collins asks three male mechanics to take a look at her engine because it is acting funny. Upon looking under the hood, one mechanic repeatedly screams, "You got no engine!" Collins agitates them by asking, "Can you just put a new one in for me?" and "Do you think my car needs a new gas line?" and then saying, "It drove just fine on Long Island." Later, Funt parks the car on a main street, and Collins asks a man to see what could be going wrong with the car. When he says it is missing an engine, Collins asks, "Do you think it fell out or is maybe in the trunk?" The laughter cultivates a sense of the female being completely in control of mobility associated with automobile cultures because of Collins' ability to prank men and play on their supposed superior mechanical knowledge. The woman finds mobility, not spatial isolation, in these skits.

OPENING SPACE THROUGH POWER GEOMETRIES IN *AN AMERICAN FAMILY*

Debuting in 1973 on PBS, *An American Family* is a twelve-episode series that captured the lives of Santa Barbara's Loud family—father Bill, mother Pat, and children Lance, Kevin, Grant, Delilah, and Michele—from May 30, 1971 to January 1, 1972. The series' meticulous documentation of locales opens space through *power geometries*. Doreen Massey theorizes power geometries as uneven power relationships based on the flow of capital, labor, citizens, transportation, and culture between two different spaces (i.e., cities, regions, or nations). Power geometries entail hegemonic control where the dominant power in one space can control the social relations in another. The geometries also afford counterhegemonic possibilities where emerging or subordinate social groups resist power structures organizing the relationship between two spaces.[22] This illuminates the politics of travel and movement that permeate *An American Family*. Jeffrey Ruoff has shown how series' producer Craig Gilbert wanted his show to capture the disintegration of the postwar family in the wake of the social upheaval of the late 1960s and early 1970s. The second wave of feminism refuted patriarchy, and the gay rights movement challenged heteronormativity.[23] I would add these challenges are mapped onto power geometries in the series. Eight of the twelve episodes involve at least one family member travelling. Travel acts as a counter-hegemonic force in *An American Family*. Sometimes the spaces to which people travel offer alternative social formations that can then be incorporated into the Loud's lives in Santa Barbara. Other times, the people left behind in Santa Barbara during travel can challenge the family's status quo.

An American Family precisely defines exterior and interior spaces through technologies and styles of Direct Cinema. Technological advances such as lightweight noiseless 16 mm cameras, portable sound equipment such as the Nagra tape recorder, and film stock for low light conditions made it possible to shoot unobtrusively and with little set-up time. Birthed in the late 1950s and early 1960s by filmmakers such as Robert Drew, Richard Leacock, D.A. Pennebaker, Allan King, and Albert Maysles, Direct Cinema documented objective reality through minimal interference of the production crew. This observational film style eschewed narrative or argument in order to capture people in unadulterated states. Producer Craig Gilbert crafted *An American Family* in this tradition. Susan Raymond, the series' sound recordist, said, "We really believed rigidly in 'fly on the wall' observation. It's a very Zen exercise to diminish your presence as best as you can."[24] With his Éclair NPR 16 mm camera, cinematographer Alan Raymond moved freely through spaces and relied on staples of Direct Cinema, such as wide shots, deep compositions, and long takes.[25] This enabled the series to highlight the different landscapes of the places family members visited, since the camera was light enough to follow the cast through the streets. For example, when Pat travels to Eugene, Oregon in Episode Four to visit her mother, Alan Raymond captures images of Pat on the plane and also includes a pan of the city surrounded by plush mountains and gray Northwestern cloud cover. Raymond later sits in the back seat of Pat's mother's car and frames shots so that towering evergreens on the side of the road mark this city as visually different from the beaches and mountains of Santa Barbara.

The long takes and wide shots document specifics of interior places to make these locales dynamic elements of a scene. Episode Two focuses on Pat's trip to New York City to visit her gay son, Lance. The opening scene in New York City is a long take of Lance in his room at the Chelsea Hotel that he shares with Soren Angenoux. While the camera holds on Lance, it captures the run-down décor—the wooden windows in need of a painting, the worn curtains, the older wallpaper beneath the windows, and the dirty white paint on the walls—that rejected middle-class norms and made the hotel a famous residence for aspiring artists. When Pat enters the hotel lobby, a wide shot captures the avant-garde art in the hotel as well as an advertisement for a production of a Sam Shepard play. Later Lance walks Pat to her room at the hotel, full of blue, dilapidated furniture. Lance says the place looks like a heroin addict went wild in it, and Pat half-jokingly says the décor makes her want to check out and go home tomorrow. The star of this part of the episode is the Chelsea Hotel itself. The conversations between Lance and Soren, and then Lance and his mother are banal. The visual details of the hotel differentiate it from the Loud home.

This aesthetic of space is evident in the opening scene of the series' premiere episode; the aesthetic combines with an onscreen narration by producer Craig Gilbert to summon inspirational notions of manifest destiny and to suggest that American notions of family associated with it died as the spaces of the West became closed. This sets the scene for complex power geometries. The opening long shot starts on the ocean and pans left to the breathtaking beach and the awe-inspiring city of Santa Barbara. The background of the shot gains visual dominance through the pan. The Santa Ynez Mountains emerge from the beach and tower over the city in the top third of the frame. The shot elicits emotions attached to manifest destiny where opportunity and natural beauty await American citizens travelling west. The scene then cuts to Gilbert standing on a hill in front of Santa Barbara, with mountains continuing to dominate the upper third of the screen. Here the coast is unnoticeable. The city, cramped and closed off, barely peaks out under the hill. Gilbert's narration troubles notions of Western openness by placing the history of Bill and Pat's family within the history of Western expansion. Gilbert recounts how Bill's and Pat's ancestors emigrated from Western Europe to the East Coast and Midwest. Both families are quintessentially American because their belief in manifest destiny brought them to the West Coast to search for better jobs and a better place to raise a family. Gilbert states the American notion of manifest destiny is falling apart now that the west is developed. Bill and Pat moved south to Santa Barbara because the family could no longer move west. The changing spatial migrations of American families accompany changing spatial relationships of the family.

The first half of the episode presents two differing views of the family, poetically created through filming the Louds on the first day and last day of the shoot. While all other eleven episodes contain a unity of time that follow a singular action of one or a few family members, Episode One begins on the last day of shooting and then rewinds seven months to 6:30 am on the first day of shooting. On that first day we see images of traditionally defined gender roles of the immediate postwar era. Pat diligently prepares a bacon and egg breakfast while her older daughter, Delilah, sets the table. The younger daughter, Michele, joins them to help. The camera's focus on little details, such as Pat flipping bacon strips and Delilah placing forks next to plates, coupled with the sounds of frying food and clanking silverware, convey traditional female domesticity. When Bill enters the kitchen, the scene presents men as professionals, artists, and moral centers of the family. Dressed in business attire, Bill asks where his keys are so he can drive to work. Son Grant enters and talks to his father about a film he just finished. Bill notes his son Kevin was up late last night practicing his music. With his knowledge of nature, Bill leads a family conversation about how the disappearing bird population in their backyard will disturb the ecosystem. The children defer to him while Pat sits quietly.

Such idealized visions of postwar gender roles ring hollow within the episode's narrative, which places these events after a twenty-minute scene of the family celebrating New Year's Eve on the last full day of shooting. Pat has filed for divorce. Bill lives in a hotel and gets ready for a date. The Loud children party with their friends in the basement of the family home. Hard rock bands such as The Who blast out while some kids smoke cigarettes, others are intoxicated, and others dance erotically. Pat remains peripheral to the party, sometimes coming to the edge of the basement to watch. Mostly she stays upstairs. The family is disconnected.

A meaningful edit in Episode One depicts Pat's alienation in the spaces of Santa Barbara. Grant gives a report on the reconstruction era in his high school history class and explains the tragedy of the time was that African Americans had been denied freedom and couldn't achieve the American dream. The episode cuts to Pat grocery shopping. The edit seems ironic at

Figure 1.2 The Louds, the stars of *An American Family*, in their Santa Barbara home.
PBS/Photofest ©PBS

first, probing if Pat's financial wellness is the type of personal fulfillment offered by the American dream. As the long take goes on, it becomes clear the episode uses the history of African American enslavement to illuminate Pat's entrapment in a traditional family. The shot captures the cramped isles of the supermarket that offer no horizon. The long takes convey the boredom of Pat and other women in the background reading nutritional labels. None of the women talk to each other, further emphasizing their isolation.

The next scene with Bill shows how men experience a spatial openness in postwar gender roles. Bill, who owns a strip-mining equipment company, is selling replacement parts at a mine. Bill joyously talks business with the other men, and the space is much more open with clear horizons. For the man, the nuclear family offers financial, professional, and social freedom. The next scene furthers this point. Bill takes Pat to a work party at an idyllic golf course. The long takes and sound capture Bill happily talking to other men in wide shots. Pat, however, is typically framed in a medium shot as she sits in a chair. There are only empty chairs near her; the tight shots visualize her emotional isolation. The sound design of the scene mutes her to capture her lack of voice. The only moments where the sound picks her up is when she talks about how she wants to open a hotel and when she implies Bill is talking to a woman because he wants to have another affair. Her isolation in the frame spatializes her unfulfilled professional desires and her marital unhappiness.

The second episode builds power geometries across Santa Barbara. Pat encounters non-normative sexual identities and lifestyles in New York City that allow her to see the confining nature of her life as a Santa Barbara housewife. In New York, Lance and Soren take Pat to La MaMa's *Vain Victory*, a camp transvestite musical. The notion of drag serves as a poignant metaphor for Pat's transformation, for she will begin to try on different identities to liberate herself from her limited socially prescribed identity. Pat's reaction after the show might initially suggest she didn't like it. She says, "Yeah, I thought it was pretty gross," "I don't like things that make me feel uncomfortable and embarrassed, and it did," and "part of the time I was bored." Wearing an upper-middle-class outfit, Pat appears as someone whose class status is not akin to enjoying drag shows. But Pat's expression of interest in the show coupled with the way she is framed and mic'd in the scene are significant. Pat says "part of the time I was amused" in a medium shot at a table that frames Lance, Pat, and Soren together. The shots and use of sound in this scene tell us that Pat has a community in New York's underground scene. The sound records her voice so that it is equally as loud as Lance's and Soren's. Pat begins to find a social group and personal fulfillment in ways that were not available in Santa Barbara.

The camp world of New York's underground to which Lance intro-duces Pat offers her various escapes from her oppression and alienation in

Santa Barbara. When Lance and Soren take her to an Andy Warhol exhibit, she is able to converse with them about the meaning of Warhol's art, an intellectual endeavor far from her focus on domestic chores in California. Moreover, Lance brings a tarot card reader to his room at the Chelsea, and the mystical practice offers Pat relief from her material oppression. The tarot reader says Pat is in for a major change in life that will bring about temporary financial hardships but will eventually lead to a better life. The tarot reader says Pat's life is an emotionally draining chore.

A scene where Lance and Pat stroll through Central Park propounds the geometric nature of spatial relations for the series. A camera follows the two from behind and captures the trees, walkways, and through streets as the two walk to the Bethesda Fountain north of 72nd Street. In a café in front of the statue, Lance asks his mother if she misses California. Pat resolutely answers, "No." This conversation is preceded by one on the walk where Pat acknowledges the differences between Santa Barbara and New York City, and says New York City is an ideal home for Lance because he could never be himself in California. Pat feels no affinity for her life in Santa Barbara, but she explains it feels awkward being in New York City without her husband. Her travel offers new ways to understand home, but offers no utopian escapism. Lance's world allows Pat to see her entrapment and gives her a voice she lacks in California. Pat will take this back with her to transform her life in Santa Barbara.

Pat's return to Santa Barbara in Episode Three constructs a power geometry for conflicting notions of masculinity and femininity. The episode contrasts Delilah's boredom in conventional femininity with Pat's post-trip exhilaration. The episode meticulously documents items of preparation for Delilah's upcoming dance recital, such as putting on makeup, trying on dance costumes, listening to dance instructors, and practicing. Delilah's boredom is reminiscent of Pat's in Episode One. Delilah is billed as a traditional mother in training. Bill tells Pat that Delilah took over the mother role while Pat was away by planning breakfasts and getting everyone ready for school. Pat, contrastingly, begins the episode with a zest for life that has grown since her time with Lance in New York. It is buttressed by her sense of professional fulfillment she gets on her trip home. Bill asks her to stop in Baltimore to speak with a parts manufacturer about future business with

Bill's company. This is the only professional work Pat does in the series. She does it with happiness and confidence. When she returns to Santa Barbara, she is joyful at lunch with Bill. She says, "Lance's world is so different. . . . After the shock wore off, it was really so fascinating. I don't think I would have had such a good time anywhere else." Bill quickly squelches Pat's exuberance by telling her she didn't sound like she was having fun on the phone and that Delilah was a great mother while Pat was gone, trying to make Pat fit properly within spatial relationships of postwar domesticity.

Episode Four spatializes residual forms of traditional family life to explain how the status quo traverses spaces such as Santa Barbara. Episode One sets up Eugene, Oregon, as a metonym for manifest destiny and familial bliss. Pat's return to Eugene in Episode Four activates this theme through nostalgia, which appears onscreen through the use of home movies shot on Super 8 film from when Lance, Grant, and Kevin were young children living in Oregon. The past looks different in this series. It's grainy, faded, and technologically simpler than the footage shot in 1971. It also sounds different. Pat speaks over images in a voiceover narration. The nondiegetic music articulates innocence to family life. Home movies from Christmas are set to a childlike version of "Jingles Bells." Films from different times play to a gentle carnival-like music. The movies show idealistic images of family. Pat reflects on how Bill was in the Army when Lance was born, and the holiday footage was the first time the couple spent together with their child, conjuring up ideologies of togetherness where leisure time functioned as family time. Pat portrays the home as idyllic when she says Kevin was clumsy while learning to walk, but the yard's soft ground always cushioned his fall.

The episode undercuts mythic notions of manifest destiny and familial harmony by showing how Eugene is being remade. This plot troubles the town's Edenic past and places it in the flows of time. Pat and Bill grew up in Victorian homes at a time when Eugene began to blossom as more Americans travelled west. As Pat tours the town with her mother, she discovers that her childhood home has been torn down. Bill's childhood home is vacant. Pat's mother notes it's a rarity to see an old house in Eugene that hasn't been bulldozed. The episode lays bare how the architecture and buildings made during the period of Western expansion are being replaced by new homes with amenities such as garages and eat-in kitchens.

When Pat visits the first home that she and Bill owned, she is upset by the area's economic downturn. The episode powerfully sets up Eugene as a space that exerts an idyllic influence on the Loud's life in Santa Barbara and then shows the complex differences between Eugene as mythic space and Eugene as a space in time.

Episodes Five and Six undercut the idealistic vision of familial togetherness mythic Eugene offers by using the family's geographic separation to convey their emotional distance. In Episode Five, Kevin travels to Australia for his father's business. Grant drives to Orange County to work a construction job for his father's friend. Lance journeys to Europe to work for a theatre company. Bill vacations in Hawaii, and Pat takes her daughters on an all-female Taos vacation. The emotional distance in the family registers in part through the children's attitudes toward their parents. While Kevin embraces his father's work opportunity, Grant resents his father for setting up the construction job. Bored with her mother's vacation, Delilah leaves a week early and takes a bus home to escape conventional notions of femininity that she finds at the Taos retreat. Episode Six unites the Louds in the same space, but suggests they are still emotionally distant from each other. Pat and Bill disagree about what their evolving relationship with the children means. Pat laments the children's increasing distance from her. Bill says he welcomes the children moving on and moving away.

Travel and power geometries structure the way Pat initiates the divorce. Although Bill frequently travels during episodes, the camera does not follow him extensively until he goes on a business trip of the Midwest, South, and Southwest during the time when Pat files for divorce in Santa Barbara. Episode Eight meticulously documents Bill's meetings at various strip mines where he tries to sell equipment. The details capture what appears to be a normal trip for Bill and show how Bill earns the money he needs to function as family patriarch. Bill's absence in Santa Barbara allows for Pat to redefine her role in this space, as she files for divorce while Bill can't exert control over her. Just as important, she takes a trip to Glendale, ninety minutes southwest of Santa Barbara, to tell her siblings about her divorce. The trip is as liberating for her as her New York trip was. Away from Santa Barbara, she expresses her pain and fears in ways that we never heard in Santa Barbara. She discusses her fears of Bill's infidelities and how he travels in order to have affairs. The scene takes place on a deck at night, leaving Pat in a space that is attached to the house, but not explicitly domestic. The space frees her to address explicitly her unhappiness in her domestic role and also recasts Bill's business trips as emotional betrayals, not financial support.

Episode Nine juxtaposes Bill's seemingly ordinary return from a business trip with Pat's life-altering announcement that she has filed for divorce, continuing the power geometry of Bill's departure leading to Pat's empowerment. Bill's shock and sorrow appears when he returns home from his business trip to get the news from Pat. The scene uses long takes in its opening to capture both the ordinariness of Bill's return and the extraordinariness of Pat's serving him with divorce papers. We begin in the driveway as Grant, who has driven Bill from the airport to their home, walks with his father into the house. The camera follows them up the stairs and into the house. Next, another long take captures Bill greeting his wife and hugging his daughter Delilah. In the same take, Delilah moves and Pat tells Bill she has filed for divorce and wants him to move out immediately. The camera, until this point, has remained in a long shot against the wall, but when Pat delivers this news, the camera zooms in on Bill to capture his surprise reaction. The next segment of the scene focuses on Bill calling local hotels and informing his business associates where to reach him. This section of the scene has the most cuts, although the cuts are meant to show ordinary events occurring as Bill makes life-changing calls. The scene cuts to the family dog scratching itself, to Pat smoking a cigarette in the other room, and to Delilah fiddling with her hands at the table. The closing three-minute long take registers the complete emptiness of Bill's life after receiving the news from Pat. There is no sound in the background, so we hear Bill taking his clothes off their hangers, packing his suitcase, opening doors, and loading up his car. The harsh audio registers the disintegration of the postwar patriarchal family. These are sounds of despair, of leaving a house offering established identities and moving into the unknown.

An American Family offers the family members' liberatory identities post-divorce paper deliverance, in large part through the power geometry created by Lance's return to Santa Barbara in Episode Eleven. Episode Ten attempts to capture the children's uneventful lives in the wake of the divorce (going back to school, playing in the family pool, etc.) while Episode Eleven sees

Lance's return offer utopian possibilities of inhabiting the space of Santa Barbara. Lance stands for movement and fluidity. During a phone call with a friend, Lance complains about the closed-mindedness of Santa Barbara residents, linking it to a lack of movement. He says, "I look at all the people here. They haven't been anywhere else. It's really awful." The friend contrasts this to Lance's extensive travels, suggesting travel allowed Lance to find fulfillment. The next scene furthers the theme of liberation and movement by editing visual footage of Lance taking a bike ride through backroads in the Santa Ynez Mountains to an audio clip of Bill reading a letter he wrote to Lance. Lance's freedom of movement foils Bill's conclusions on the imprisoning nature of the postwar nuclear family. The camera is seemingly mounted on the back of a vehicle to capture Lance's ride in a long shot with steady framing. This is the only extended shot we see of any of the Louds moving through Santa Barbara. Bill's letter attacks postwar notions of togetherness, explicitly saying it forces people to spend all of their time with their family and makes familial relationships unpleasant. Bill suggests that families would be a much better unit if they were loosely structured. Bill then talks about how he loves Pat and calls her his Rock of Gibraltar. The metaphor turns marriage into an immovable force, which contrasts Lance's joyous motion on screen as he rides his bike in a camp manner, singing, and bobbing his head. The letter is quite touching in the way Bill claims that moving forward he wants to be genuine friends with Lance and not simply a paternal authority figure. The episode ends with a freeze fame of Lance and Bill posing for a picture, which seems to embrace their new image of friendship. The last time we see Bill in the series—in Episode Twelve—he is talking to his friend about how the American notion of family chokes any real and sincere relationships you can have with your children. Bill's turn to Lance as a sincere friend is different than the relationship he has with any of his other children. Lance also brings a fluidity to the way he and his sisters relate. He does Delilah's makeup to make her look goth. Later Lance trades beauty product tips with Michele and gives her a feminine sweater of his to wear. The typical roles of male and female that resulted in Pat and Bill's unhappiness break down when Lance returns.

The series closes with Pat in her house talking to two other friends, one of whom is also going through a divorce, to show how much Pat's spatial relations have changed throughout the course of the series. The scene frames the three friends individually and pans to capture the friends when they talk. Whereas Pat's individualized framing in the first episode showed her alienation, her new framing shows her confidence and independence. She smiles and jokes as she talks about the painful process of dividing assets and calculating alimony. When her friend tells Pat this is a depressing conversation, she laughs and says, "But these things happen," with the camera freeze framing on her smiling face. Pat's happiness speaks to the way the series opened Santa Barbara through power geometries that brought in feminist and gay knowledge and critiqued nostalgic notions of family togetherness.

Despite *An American Family*'s focus on the spatial dynamics of the postwar family, it still managed to be part of a larger culture of postwar economic egalitarianism, both through the way it was part of PBS's cultural mission and through the way that the family was portrayed as American and not classed. Laurie Ouellette chronicles how the rise of PBS in the late 1960s was shaped by a larger postwar ethos of cultural and economic egalitarianism. Discourse about the rise of public television identified the way that people's cultural knowledge was shaped by their social class. Those in a higher economic bracket have access to education that cultivates cultural sophistication. But in the late 1960s and early 1970s, American education sought to level these social distinctions by making education more accessible to the working class. More people attended universities in order to earn middleclass salaries and gain sophisticated cultural knowledge. Similarly, there was a larger cultural discourse that public television could bring high culture to the masses and grant them the same cultural knowledge as the elite. This defined public television against commercial television, making the former good TV and positioning the latter as bad. With *An American Family*, PBS invested in a series that would familiarize its viewers with the latest artistic trends in documentary filmmaking and increase their knowledge of cinematic styles.

An American Family also resonated with postwar economic egalitarianism through the way the Loud family became emblematic of the national state of families. The Loud family, despite being wealthy, were meant to symbolize the general disintegration of the American family after the social unrest of the late 1960s. Episodes never highlight how the Louds could afford luxuries that most families could not. Rather, the program stressed commonalities between the Louds and viewers. Bill was a rich entrepreneur, but his daughters took dance lessons. Two of his sons played in a rock band. His other son aspired to be a bohemian artist. His children played in the back yard and went to school just like ordinary children. Part of what enabled this at this historical moment is that capital was distributed more evenly across all economic classes, so a majority of Americans could still afford a home, take vacations, and pay for their children's sports and leisure activities. Even though the Louds are wealthy, they are typical.

Although authorship is not a main focus of this chapter or this book, it's worth noting that *An American Family*'s reliance on the style and philosophy of Direct Cinema shifted reality television away from the authored world of Allen Funt to an authorless world where cast members became more known than producers. Funt played such a large role on *Candid Camera* that he publicly appeared as the program's author in several ways. He cohosted the studio segments, he frequently played the role of provocateur, and the opening credits introduced Allen Funt as "Mr. *Candid Camera*." *Candid Camera*'s goal to capture ordinary people in extraordinary situations required an author to push the sketch into a new realm of possibility. Direct Cinema effaced the identity of the filmmaker to convey reality objectively. Moving this film style from the film theatres to television screens required some negotiations. Gilbert appears on camera at the beginning of the premiere episode to set up the premise of the series. He also uses one voice over in the opening of each episode to explain to viewers the background for events. Apart from these brief moments, Gilbert disappears so that his series can show the Louds.

THE GENTRIFIED NEIGHBORHOOD AS TRANSPORTATION HUB: OPEN SPACE ON MTV'S *THE REAL WORLD*, SEASON ONE

Unlike other grandparents or parents of reality television, *The Real World* pre-dates the twenty-first-century reality television boom and is also a part of it. When *The Real World* premiered in 1992, MTV promoted it as a docu-soap, not reality television. Producers Jonathan Murry and Mary-Ellis Bunim wanted a series that mixed the seriousness of Direct Cinema with the intensely emotional plots and the serial narratives of soaps. As MTV continued to renew *The Real World* (as of 2016, *The Real World* is still in production), the series became relabeled as reality television. *The Real World* is also a unique forerunner to reality television because it aired once cities had been redefined from industrial centers requiring the residence of all classes to post-industrial financial centers that catered to the elite. Moreover, the first season of *The Real World* filmed seven strangers living in New York City's SoHo neighborhood, a newly gentrified neighborhood. Despite this, the first season of MTV's *The Real World* is an example of what Raymond Williams calls a *residual culture*. Season One holds industrial beliefs that cities belong to all classes. It attacks the way space operates in gentrified areas. Daniel Rosensweig argues gentrified areas are closed spaces that insure non-privileged classes and races are kept at bay so that the financially fortunate can live and spend leisure time in "safe spaces." The gentrified area also functions as a magnet for other privileged citizens who come to the area for entertainment.[26] *The Real World* changes the spatial operation of gentrification and opens space by transforming a gentrified neighborhood from a privileged tourist destination to a transportation hub to a region that suffers from racism, poverty, and sexism.

    The Real World held on to dated views of urban space partly because MTV branded itself against the political regime that helped to deregulate the economy and transform cities into homes for the elite. Andrew Goodwin argues that MTV created a liberal brand in the mid- to late-1980s by airing videos from leftist artists such as R.E.M., Public Enemy, U2, Bruce Springsteen, Lou Reed, and Living Colour; by campaigning for the ethical treatment of animals; and by humanizing people suffering from HIV and AIDS. The channel consciously worked African American rights and culture into its brand to challenge the racist social surround and to correct previous perceptions that it was a racist channel. For the first year and a half of its existence, MTV aired only white music videos. Executives justified such racism on the preferences of their market, claiming its predominantly white audience wanted to watch videos by white musicians. Many black artists protested the white-only policy, and Michael Jackson and his record company defeated it when they threatened to pull all of the company's videos from MTV if the channel didn't air Jackson's videos for "Thriller," "Billie Jean," and "Beat It." MTV's rebrand aggressively eliminated stigmas of being racist by creating black music shows such as *Yo! MTV Raps*; airing cutting-edge, politically controversial music videos such as Public Enemy's "By the Time I Get to Arizona," where the band assassinates white officials in Arizona, a state that failed to celebrate Martin Luther King Jr. Day; and supporting a Free James Brown Campaign when the artist was jailed on drug charges.[27]

These were bold branding initiatives at a time when the Republican Party attacked many social justice initiatives of the 1960s and 1970s by representing socially disempowered groups as bad citizens who abuse government subsidies. During his presidency, Ronald Reagan demonized African Americans as welfare abusers, drug addicts, gang members, and bad family members. Reagan and other Republicans tried to dismantle Affirmative Action, believing that it created reverse discrimination against whites. Reaganism placed faith in the patriarchal white nuclear family and felt that it could make America strong again by emphasizing a hard work ethic.[28] This intersected with the political moment's broader assault on the poor and the backlash against feminism.

MTV's branding goals became mapped onto the politics of space on *The Real World*; Season One follows people leaving gentrified SoHo to have a deeper understanding of problems of race, class, and gender throughout the city and region. In Episode Eleven, Kevin travels to his hometown of Jersey City with his girlfriend so she can understand how the neighborhood shaped him. The segment humanizes residents of Jersey City, one of the poorest black cities in America. Kevin runs into his life-long friend Eric. The footage shows Eric walking with his kids and playing football with them, which counters Reagan's views of poor African Americans as irresponsible fathers, gang members, and drug addicts. Spliced-in confessionals contextualize the struggle for human dignity against the harshness of the economic system. Kevin notes, "You know, he's a survivor, like, that's the thing. He's just surviving." Kevin's disgusted facial expression shows his hatred of the effects of poverty on the human spirit. When Kevin and his girlfriend first arrive, the camera captures boarded up, condemned buildings covered in graffiti. We also see an arrest made when several cop cars descend on a building known for drug dealing and prostitution. Kevin explains how his mother saved money to leave the neighborhood because of the prevalence of crime that accompanies such destitute neighborhoods. The trip from SoHo to Jersey City documents Kevin's sympathies for poor African Americans experiencing the brutality of capitalism.

Another part of the episode follows Kevin from SoHo to his poetry reading at the Nuyorican Poets Café in the East Village to show how his cultural production is shaped by his commitment to black politics. In "Mental Terrorism," he blasts popular culture for enslaving African Americans through harmful images that have material effects on the economic wellness of a social group. This episode demonstrates the two main destinations for cast members once they leave the transportation hub of SoHo: they go to a neighborhood

Figure 1.3 The cast members of Season One of *The Real World* in their SoHo loft.
MTV/Photofest ©MTV

written out of the imaginary of a post-industrial capitalist city or they go to cultural production venues that allow cast members to speak about problems affecting people during the Reagan–Bush era.

An example of the former occurs in Episode Nine when Andre and Julie walk to a "Reaganville"—a group of homeless people living together—at the 79th Street Boat Basin. Julie befriends an African American homeless woman, Darlene. We learn a lot about the struggles of homeless people from Darlene. She teaches Julie about the Midnight Run, a nonprofit that brings food and clothes to the homeless. There are heartbreaking conversations between Julie and Darlene, like when Julie asks Darlene what her plans are. Darlene says, "I've been trying to look into an apartment, but it's hard to find one. Because I'm on the welfare, and my welfare only allows me $215 for rent, and an apartment, it's like one room I need, and it's like $425 a month." Julie asks, "What are you supposed to do?" Darlene responds, "That's what I want to know." When Darlene talks, she's articulate and confident in her explanations of the system's faults. Julie later spends the night at the Reaganville. The homeless people she meets in this episode are hardly the bad citizens and welfare abusers Reagan made them out to be. They are sincere people victimized by the social system.

The other strategy of travel, going to spaces of cultural production, shapes the way Heather B. articulates black feminism in Episode Two. When Heather travels to the recording studio, she takes Julie with her, and this location becomes an alternative location to express social injustices. Heather B. was a member of the social activist rap group Boogie Down Productions from the South Bronx. She was cast for *The Real World* when she left the group to start a solo career. Episode Two has Heather travel to a New York recording studio to produce an album with Kenny Parker, a member of Boogie Down Productions. Heather's album is titled "The System Sucks," which rails against the social system and also addresses issues important to women such as date rape. When she records her rap about date rape, Heather rages against the horrors that women can face with lines like, "I wish I had my gun/I would have shot him dead./But we filled out the papers./And left instead./Could you believe that?/Just our luck./I just say to myself, 'the system sucks'." Like Kevin, Heather goes to spaces reserved for black artists, but she does so to express what it means to be a black woman.

A look at travel in Julie's evolving relationship with Kevin and Heather demonstrates the realism of The Real World. The first wave of scholarship about MTV music videos surfaced in the mid-1980s and argued they employed a postmodern aesthetic by fusing high art with popular culture, by creating texts that were intertextual, and by using an intertextuality that blurred history, chronology, and cultural forms.[29] This hyper-stylized aesthetic was seen as the opposite of realism's transparency and simplicity, but it came to shape the perception of reality on The Real World. As a docu-soap, The Real World blended elements of direct cinema's fly-on-the-wall aesthetic with the soap opera's intensely emotional plots that stretched across the season in a serial narrative. Julie's rising awareness of black culture shows how these two styles come together to create realism. I have written about a common narrative trajectory on early seasons of The Real World where a naïve white person from the country will make a racist statement that concerns African American roommates, but the series suggests racism can be overcome through interpersonal relationships that start when African Americans teach the naïve white about black culture, and the learning process turns into a sincere friendship that eradicates racism. These plots are highly emotional and soap-ish, often stretching from the first episode to the last.[30] Much of Julie's transformation takes place while travelling away from SoHo. After Julie expresses racism when she assumes Heather having a beeper must mean she is a drug dealer (which assumes that if you are black and have a beeper you are criminal), Heather and Kevin take Julie to another part of the city to discuss stereotypes of African Americans. This begins a learning process for Julie. Heather takes Julie to recording sessions. She takes Julie to East Rutherford, New Jersey so they can meet African American basketball star Larry Johnson. Kevin applauds Julie's trips to the Reaganville, and Julie travels to NYU to see Kevin teach as an adjunct instructor. While the SoHo loft serves as a home base to Julie, Heather, and Kevin, Julie's learning comes through the African American cast members continuously exposing her to black culture in other parts of the city.

Space slowly transformed on The Real World over the course of the 1990s and into the early 2000s. Seasons Two and Three, Los Angeles and San Francisco, continue to use the house as a transportation hub for travel (to AIDS awareness marches in the city of San Francisco and to the Miami home of Pedro, who was afflicted with AIDS while he was on the show). In Season Four, London work visa regulations complicated casting Americans established in their careers, so more American college students were cast. With no set work connection to the city, house members spent an unprecedented amount of time in the London house, resulting in few interesting story lines. Producers then began to cast people less established in their careers and gave them jobs for the season that would push them into the city. Season Six, Boston, had the cast working at a youth center. While these seasons felt like there was less organic travel through the city, the jobs required house members to engage in a form of social justice outside of the house.

The 2002 Las Vegas season drastically changed the representation of space on the series. Space became closed, gentrified, and/or highly commercialized. Producers set this season in the Palms Casino Resort in Las Vegas. The cast members live in the penthouse and work in clubs in the Palms. The season became a giant ad for the casino, and house members rarely left the casino. Space became increasingly commercialized on the series as the channel needed to find new ways to air and sell music. With the arrival of YouTube, the increasing prevalence of original series on MTV, and the normalization of a la carte digital technologies for listening to music, music videos and programs that only aired music videos on MTV became obsolete. To continue to find ways to sell music to its viewers, MTV began to feature popular music in original reality programs. This affected the representation of space on The Real World in the 2000s. Episodes devoted time to getting ready to go to a club and then to dancing at one. Producers flashed the name of the song in the scene in the lower right corner so that viewers could pay to download it. As a result, the Las Vegas house stopped being a transportation hub and became a dressing room to get ready for a closed space of a club used to sell music.

CONCLUSION

The closing of space on The Real World in the late 1990s and early 2000s was mirrored by the rise of police reality shows in the late 1980s and 1990s. While The Real World challenged the right's views about minorities during the Reagan–Bush era, programs such as COPS (1989–present) became a perfect televisual vehicle to visualize contemporary beliefs about post-industrial urban life and new discourses about race. Elayne Rapping argues that COPS is indicative of a shift in criminal policies where non-violent criminals were incarcerated at a higher rate than before in order to fill cells in the expanding private prison business. Most people prosecuted for these crimes were minorities and poor people. COPS avoids probing the humanity of criminals and instead labels them as deviants. Crime on this series became reduced to drug abuse, sexual deviancy, and illegal immigration. These populations are policed by typically white police officers. COPS robs cities of any dynamic employment of space where social relationships can be altered. Moreover, COPS shoots on the outskirts of the city in lands of endless highways and strip malls; no city is brought to life through its unique characteristics. Cities are generic spaces where non-whites must be policed. The city is not a place to welcome class and racial diversity; it is a space where dominant powers need to exert control and make the city into its own image.[31]

COPS shows reality television coming to terms with the policed spaces of social expulsions, but reality television's need to police the closed spaces of contemporary cities would be short lived. As Saskia Sassen argues, urban expulsions gained monumental force in the twenty-first century. Messages that the city needed to be protected from the criminal poor now rang hollow, given that most people no longer could afford to live in global cities within the United States. Now reality television had a new, very difficult task to tackle in terms of its spatial politics: it had to win our consent so that we accepted the closed residential areas of America's global cities. These complex negotiations make up the rest of the book.

NOTES

1 Kent C. Ryden, *Mapping the Invisible Landscape: Folklore, Writing, and a Sense of Place* (Iowa City, IA: University of Iowa Press, 1993), 16.

2 Allen Funt with Philip Reed, *Candidly, Allen Funt: A Million Smiles Later* (New York: Barricade, 1994), 47–8.

3 Allen Funt, *Eavesdroppers at Large: Adventures in Human Nature with Candid Mike and Candid Camera* (New York: Vanguard, 1952), 173–8.

4 Allen Funt with Philip Reed, *Candidly, Allen Funt: A Million Smiles Later* (New York: Barricade, 1994), 42.

5 See Lawrence Levine, *Highbrow/Lowbrow: The Emergence of Cultural Hierarchy in America* (Cambridge, MA: Harvard University Press, 1990).

6 Armina Marshall, "The Theatre Guild on Radio and Television," in Norman Nadel, ed., *A Pictorial History of the Theatre Guild with Special Material from Lawrence Langer and Armina Marshall* (New York: Crown, 1969), 211.

7 Jon Kraszewski, *The New Entrepreneurs: An Institutional History of Television Anthology Writers* (Middletown, CT: Wesleyan University Press, 2010), 70–102.

8 Allen Funt with Philip Reed, *Candidly, Allen Funt: A Million Smiles Later* (New York: Barricade, 1994), 13–16.

9 Allen Funt with Philip Reed, *Candidly, Allen Funt: A Million Smiles Later* (New York: Barricade, 1994), 14.

10 C. Wright Mills, *White Collar: The American Middle Classes* (New York: Oxford University Press, 1951); David Reisman with Nathaniel Glazer and Reuel Denney, *The Lonely Crowd* (New Haven, CT: Yale University Press, 1950); William H. Whyte, Jr., *The Organization Man* (New York: Doubleday, 1957); John Keats, *The Crack in the Picture Window* (New York: Houghton Mifflin, 1956).

11 Leonard B. Stern, "*Marty*, Broadway Hit, Written by Clintonite, '39," *Clinton News*, May 6, 1955.

12 Paddy Chayefsky, *Television Plays* (New York: Simon and Schuster, 1955), 173.

13 Allen Funt with Philip Reed, *Candidly, Allen Funt: A Million Smiles Later* (New York: Barricade, 1994), 45.

14 Allen Funt with Philip Reed, *Candidly, Allen Funt: A Million Smiles Later* (New York: Barricade, 1994), 28.

15 Allen Funt with Philip Reed, *Candidly, Allen Funt: A Million Smiles Later* (New York: Barricade, 1994), 11.

16 http://www.merriam-webster.com/dictionary/prescription. Accessed April 3, 2015.

17 Arthur Miller, "Tragedy and the Common Man," in Robert A. Martin, ed., *The Theatre Essays of Arthur Miller* (New York: Viking, 1977), 4.

18 Arthur Miller, "Tragedy and the Common Man," in Robert A. Martin, ed., *The Theatre Essays of Arthur Miller* (New York: Viking, 1977), 5.

19 Harold Sampson, Sheldon L. Messinger, and Robert Towne, *Schizophrenic Women: Studies in Marital Crisis* (New York: Atherton Press, 1964), 128.

20 Carol A.B. Warren, *Madwives: Schizophrenic Women in the 1950s* (New Brunswick, NJ: Rutgers University Press, 1987), 58.

21 Virginia Scharff, *Taking the Wheel, Women and the Coming of the Motor Age* (Albuquerque, NM: University of New Mexico Press, 1992), 172.

22 See Doreen Massey, *World City* (Malden, MA: Polity, 2007), 97–129; Arun Saldanha, "Power Geometry as Philosophy of Space," in David Featherstone and Joe Painter, eds, *Spatial Politics: Essays for Doreen Massey* (Malden, MA: Wiley-Blackwell, 2013), 44–55.

23 Jeffrey Ruoff, *An American Family: A Televised Life* (Minneapolis, MN: University of Minnesota Press, 2002), 6–23.

24 Quoted in Jeffrey Ruoff, *An American Family: A Televised Life* (Minneapolis, MN: University of Minnesota Press, 2002), xxi.

25 Jeffrey Ruoff, *An American Family: A Televised Life* (Minneapolis, MN: University of Minnesota Press, 2002), 31, 33.

26 Daniel Rosensweig, *Retro Ball Parks: Instant History, Baseball, and the New American City* (Knoxville, TN: University of Tennessee Press, 2005), 113–42.

27 Andrew Goodwin, "Fatal Distractions: MTV Meets Postmodern Theory," in Simon Frith, Andrew Goodwin, and Lawrence Grossberg, eds, *Sound and Vision: The Music Video Reader* (New York: Routledge, 1992), 62–3.

28 Herman Gray, *Watching Race: Television and the Struggle for "Blackness"* (Minneapolis, MN: University of Minnesota Press, 1995), 57–69.

29 Andrew Goodwin, "Fatal Distractions: MTV Meets Postmodern Theory," in Simon Frith, Andrew Goodwin, and Lawrence Grossberg, eds, *Sound and Vision: The Music Video Reader* (New York: Routledge, 1992), 45–6.

30 Jon Kraszewski, "Country Hicks and Urban Cliques: Mediating Race, Reality, and Liberalism on MTV's The Real World," in Susan Murray and Laurie Ouellette, eds, *Reality TV: Remaking Television Culture*, 2nd edition (New York: New York University Press, 2009), 205–22.

31 Elayne Rapping, "Aliens, Nomads, Mad Dogs, and Road Warriors: The Changing Face of Criminal Violence on TV," in Susan Murray and Laurie Ouellette, eds, *Reality TV: Remaking Television Culture*, 1st edition (New York: New York University Press, 2004), 214–30.

2

DIASPORIC NOSTALGIA AND THE FRACTURED GEOGRAPHIES OF TWENTY-FIRST-CENTURY URBAN REALITY TELEVISION

Real urban space continues to be a hallmark of reality television in the twenty-first century, even though the class make-up of American cities has undergone a profound transformation. Our cities, once industrial centers of manufacturing that housed and employed a range of social classes—from unskilled manual laborers to educated white-collar executives—survived obsolescence at the start of deindustrialization through a political economy of social expulsions that remade cites into crucial points in a network of global capitalism. Now, elite financiers live in cities and rely on a servant class to prepare their food, clean their clothes, walk their dogs, and take on a variety of other tasks done within the family during the post-World War II era. Cities are now closed residential and leisure spaces, with a lack of employment options and soaring costs of living barring most people from residing there. This is an economic environment worthy of the word sociologist Saskia Sassen uses to describe it: *brutal*.

This transformation has profoundly affected the politics of space on reality television. Rather than opening spatial relationships of economic egalitarianism in cities, like in the twentieth century, reality television programs now win our consent of closed spatial relationships in the twenty-first century. One way that this happens is by appealing to structures of nostalgia that occur when people have lost their homeland. When a significant number of middle-, working-, and lower-class people started being driven out of cities in the 1980s, they didn't leave ideas about former homes behind. Instead, they carried older notions of home with them to their new places of residence. Sociologist Zygmunt Bauman calls this phenomenon "liquid modernity," a time when residual forms of community are both untenable and comforting.[1] People in America who chose to move or who were expelled from urban regions carried concepts of home that resembled those of *global diasporas*. The term typically denotes notions of home for oppressed social groups such as Africans or Jews who were forcibly dispersed across the world. John Durham Peters argues that diaspora mediates between two conflicting notions of home. The first is *exile*, the notion that home is a primordial place that defines us and that is impossible to reconnect with. The second is *nomadism*, a belief that home is on the go with us and is constituted by hybridity, flux, and change.[2] As nomadism becomes typical within America during the age of expulsions, yearnings for lost primordial urban homes accompany this new identity. Reality television mediates former notions of home identities for Americans who have seen residential life in urban centers become unachievable.

Svetlana Boym contends the diasporic imagination is often shaped by nostalgia for a past place and time.[3] Not coincidentally, the popularity of cities on twenty-first-century reality television coincides with a monumental shift in the relationship between time and space in the genre. Whereas spatial configurations of industrial America on reality television featured the present (i.e., equality should be fought for now) or the future (i.e., the changing social relationships on a series can lead to space opening soon), the geographic constructions of post-industrial America on reality television often long for the past. This claim might surprise some readers who think that drama is the main television genre to address issues of the past. *Deadwood* (2004–06), *Boardwalk Empire* (2010–14), *Masters of Sex* (2013–present), and *Mad Men* (2007–15) meticulously recreate details about eras in American history. In comparison, urban reality shows such as *The Apprentice* (2004–present), *The Real Housewives* (2006–present), *Flipping Out* (2007–present), *The Amazing Race* (2001–present), and *Pitbulls and Parolees* (2009–present) appear to be about contemporary America. This rings true only if viewers believe that the past is accessible through detailed recreations. Current work in media studies and cultural studies provides a more nuanced view about the past, nostalgia, and memory. Michael Dwyer argues that "pop nostalgia can be prompted by tropes, symbols, or styles, even without claims for historical verisimilitude."[4] This is exactly how residual urbanisms exist on reality television. Real cities, which now function through systems of global financing whose complexities are incomprehensible to many viewers, become places on reality television mediated through nostalgic tropes and storylines about business practices, class relationships, and family structures associated with industrial capitalism.

Contemporary urban reality series often have visuals, sounds, and plots that work separately to summon different moments of industrial history and class politics within city spaces. These programs fracture the cultural geography of cities, presenting them simultaneously as the exclusive cities of today and the inclusive cities of the industrial era. This fracturing structures yearning in an audience made up of many people who no longer have access to residential life in the city. Boym contends that diasporic nostalgia is reflective as opposed to restorative. *Reflective nostalgia* sees the past in fractured images, as ruins that rest in new built environments. These objects function as ghosts from another time that float through the present. (*Restorative nostalgia*, conversely, recreates the past full scale.[5]) On many contemporary urban reality shows, the city's present and past class identities appear through different formal elements. The visual aesthetics of the city on these shows portray urban spaces as exclusive, luxurious, and closed, but sound—specifically the accents of cast members—and plots haunt contemporary urban space with the class equality industrial economies offered. While viewers might see contemporary cities, the programs let them long for a different period of urban economic history through what they hear and how they comprehend the story. The ultimate popularity of these shows might stem from their inability to contain their affective responses to and historical representations of the city within their separate formal elements; this is a tactic that wins our consent of the political economy of social expulsions by allowing us to feel that the cities of today are as open as they were in the mid-twentieth century.

THE SPECTICALITY OF THE CLOSED CITY ON REALITY TELEVISION

Outside space in contemporary cities exists in moments of spectacle on reality television. The term *spectacle*, as opposed to *visual*, *optic*, or *ocular*, provides a useful framework to understand how the closed nature of current urban space appears on our screens. Television studies scholars imported the term *spectacle* from film studies to develop aesthetic analysis. The most popular use of the term comes from scholars such as John T. Caldwell, Jeremy Butler, and Brett Mills, who claim the spectacular visual style of contemporary television lends it cinematic qualities.[6] Here spectacle designates a converging visual style between film and television. I draw on a different intellectual heritage of the term in film studies. Scholars such as Laura Mulvey and Tom Gunning note that spectacles operate by different logics, politics, and temporal rhythms than narratives.[7] In "Visual Pleasure and Narrative Cinema," Mulvey contends that the plot, driven by male agents solving problems, slows down for the spectacle, where women exist to be looked at and men bear the gaze. When we treat spectacles as non-narrative moments where awe structures certain political positions in the audience, we see how urban reality television shows present the closed spaces of contemporary cities as objects of wonder. Even though cities are defining features of twenty-first-century reality shows, outdoor city spaces rarely appear in the episodes. When they do, it is mostly through montages, car rides, or exterior shots to set up where an indoor scene will take place. The removal of these moments from the plot subtly constructs urban beauty in ways that align our sympathies with closed spaces.

Spectacular montages of cities on reality shows exist apart from the plot and also transition us within the plot, either from the opening credits to the first scene, from a commercial break to a scene, or from scene to scene. Montages include long shots and extreme long shots of downtowns, parks, and highways. These segments typically show exclusive areas of cities. Montages on *The Real Housewives of Beverly Hills* (2010–present) include shots of Rodeo Drive. Montages on *The Apprentice* use shots of Wall Street. Here, the city's neighborhoods never become places in which social politics are contested through spatial relationships in the story.

The visual style of these segments mirrors the class politics of poor doors mentioned in the introductory chapter whereby elite space is constructed to keep the poor at bay. Downtown Los Angeles is featured in montages in programs such as *The Real Housewives of Beverly Hills*, *Flipping Out*, and *The Hills* (2006–10). From a distance, all we see are the skyscrapers of downtown amidst a sea of concrete. Most of these buildings were constructed in the 1980s when the area went through a renaissance. The extreme long shots fail to register any poverty. We never see downtown Los Angeles' Skid Row with its 3,000–6,000 homeless residents. We never move through space to see that downtown neighbors South Central, a historically poor African American part of the city. The use of motion in the montage eradicates the poor from cities; motion surfaces not by the camera moving through city space but by cutting from one image to the next. The cut from downtown to the freeway to the park eliminates poor areas from the show. Los Angeles is merely beautiful.

The music playing during these fast-paced montages makes urban space utopian. Often set to upbeat pop music, the montages use fast-paced beats to make the city burst with energy and transform these spaces of exclusivity, brutality, and inhumanity into something fun and entertaining. These segments function the way songs do in a musical. Richard Dyer argues that song offers a utopian escape from the troubled world of narratives in films. Things go magically well in the musical numbers in ways that they never could in the story, where people experience hardships.[8] Similarly, the pop music montages of cities on reality shows present an urban world free from all problems. The beauty of the city is matched by the joy of the beat. These segments allow us to experience pleasures of the sanitized city through our senses. The awe of the image opens our eyes, and the sound of the music pulses through our bodies.

Other uses of music during the montage naturalize a social Darwinist view of the twenty-first-century city or transform the city into a place of relaxation. Some reality shows use booming orchestral music during urban montages. *The Apprentice* often uses horns and strings playing music on the lower sound registers to accompany shots of Trump Towers, the financial district, the Manhattan Skyline, and Central Park. The sound adds a ferociousness to these iconic places, making it known that only cut-throat financers survive here. At the same time, the music is uplifting through the way it starts in the lower registers and then crescendos. It aurally and viscerally sucks us in at the bottom of the musical scale and pushes us to the top to embrace the promises of capitalism. The Real Housewives franchise, however, plays light-hearted theme music with a relaxed sophistication matching the visuals of elite areas. The airy music makes the city seem like an open space, as ethereal tones make us feel like we could float through these exclusionary areas.

The city also surfaces in segments with car rides. The walks through cities on twentieth-century reality television—Lance and Pat Loud walking through Central Park on An American Family (1973), Kevin and his girlfriend walking through Jersey City on The Real World (1992)—have been replaced with the ride, and very limited types of rides: rides between work locations, rides between expensive homes and work, and rides between expensive homes and restaurants or clubs. Sometimes shows such as The Apprentice include extreme long shots from above looking down on congested streets before cutting to the inside of the car. Other programs such as The Real Housewives and Chrisley Knows Best (2014–present) begin segments in cars without establishing a larger exterior space. A standard shooting device is for the camera person to be next to the person talking so that the shot captures the urban space through the window on the opposite side. The car window shields the cast members from interacting with various social groups and instead provides direct transportation from one elite area to another, making sure to edit out poverty from urban space. The car window literally frames urban space to be looked at and guarantees the image never becomes a space in which contradictory social relationships collide.

The removal of the city from spatial relationships also occurs through the way the exteriors of houses and apartment buildings appear in the spectacle. These exteriors surface numerous times in an episode and suggest a transition from the general city locale of the montage to an interior scene at a cast member's home. While the interior of the home in American culture is often imagined as a retreat from public worlds into private spaces, the exteriors of homes occupy public spaces and are part of dynamic neighborhoods. But the exteriors of residences on reality television rip the home from its larger social context (the city) and stunt the movement of spatial relationships.

For example, Los Angeles homes are often shot from within the gated properties. Long shots register awe for both the mansion and its manicured grounds. New York town homes or apartment buildings are tightly framed within long shots so the image is only the building. We see neither commerce nor people on the streets. In these shots wealth exists in solitude, detached from the larger spaces of the city, a visual trope that reserves city space only for the elite. This tradition is carried on somewhat in real-estate programs such as *House Hunters* (1999–present), which might expand the framing of a downtown condo to show its block in order to highlight the beauty of a slightly larger surround. The real-estate program uses simplistic, almost hand-drawn maps to give a general sense of where a home is located in a city. But the information provided in the voiceover narration while the map appears is so superficial (i.e., "this home is a twenty-minute commute to where the buyer works") that it remains impossible to place a home within a larger set of spatial relationships.

As spectacles, the cities become largely interchangeable. Cities stand less as actual places with unique histories and local cultures and more as generic spaces that offer us insight into any American city. While we might see some local cultures—such as summer in the Hamptons on *The Real Housewives of New York City* (2008–present) or a competition at the Fort Worth Stock Yards on *The Amazing Race*—these themes are not as powerful as the general notion that cities are spectacles of wealth and opulence. Cities never become dynamic spaces with neighborhoods based on ethnic identities. When we see places such as SoHo on *The Real Housewives of New York City*, we never learn about the history of that neighborhood. Rather, it becomes a site of luxury residences just like Beverly Hills, Atlanta, or Miami.

SOCIAL INTIMACY AND NOSTALGIA FOR POSTWAR CLASS EQUALITY: THE SOUNDS OF THE CITY AND SHOW PREMISES

Reality shows convince us that these closed spaces serve our interests through nostalgia. Boym contends that intimacy is a crucial aspect of diasporic nostalgia. The closeness of social, familial, and geographic bonds is missing for the displaced, but they remember what it was like and where such intimacies occurred. Thus, intimacy becomes something shared by a dispersed population through memory and imagination, not through face-to-face communication. Home becomes what Sigmund Freud calls the Heimlich, that which is close and personal. Yet Heimlich is directly related to Unheimlich—the uncanny, the otherworldly. The diasporic imagination sees the ghosts of home lurking amidst the present day locales.[9] As impersonal as the spectacle of cities can be on reality shows—for all the ways that it arrests the flow of spatial relationships and reduces the city to cold, isolated images—the sounds and plots about city life summon histories of when cities were open to all social classes and constituted by the labor and immigration of the working class. The sounds and the premises work together to create an intimate city, one where a closeness between classes and families is sprinkled throughout the sterile images of the city, convincing us that the bonds that once existed in these spaces are still there for us.

The sounds we hear on urban reality shows are the sounds of an older city. Programs set in New York City such as The Apprentice and The Real Housewives of New York cast people with local accents. While this might seem like a predictable outcome of local shoots, it constructs an intimacy between classes that no longer exists in New York. The New York City accent is a classed accent, one that registers the way different ethnic and racial dialects meshed together to produce a distinct sound during a moment of industrial history when the city was open to all classes. Linguist Michael Newman argues the New York City accent marks someone from the working or middle class. The city's upper class distanced itself from this way of speaking. Indexicality—the way language marks our identity—encouraged financially successful New Yorkers to distinguish themselves socially and culturally through standardized speech.[10] But Linguist Dan Kauffman argues the New York City accent is disappearing as the city becomes enmeshed in a luxury economy. Upper-class people around the country typically speak the same grammatically-correct, proper English. Manhattan is particularly susceptible to seeing its accent disappear through the concomitant expulsion of the working and middle classes and the influx of highly educated outsiders.[11] The political economy of social expulsions is a threat to a mode of New York City speech that thrived when all classes inhabited urban space during the industrial era.

Heather Quinlan's 2008 documentary about New York City accents, *If These Knishes Could Talk*, beautifully explores how some sounds—turning an /o/ to an /aw/ (*coffee* pronounced *caw-fee*), exaggerating /ou/, pronouncing /str/ as /schtr/, losing an r after a vowel (*water* pronounced *waudah*), pronouncing /t/ as /d/, dropping the r, etc.—are no longer part of the city proper. Quinlan shows how, as Manhattan and parts of the outer boroughs become unaffordable for the working classes, the New York City accent is being pushed into parts of New Jersey, Pennsylvania, and Long Island. In a moving part of the film, Quinlan asks New York-born film director Amy Heckerling what she thinks when she hears a New York City accent today. Heckerling says, "I feel nostalgic for when I was young in New York but also for when my father was young, and I watch old movie footage of the city, I feel like a nostalgia for ghosts, essentially." The metaphor frames the sounds of the accent in a reflective nostalgia where older speech patterns are sprinkled amidst the new city, reminding people of how New York used to be.

Given the history that these sounds carry, it's hugely important that reality television stars such as Jill Zarin and Bethenny Frankel on *The Real Housewives of New York City*, Buddy Valastro on *Cake Boss* (2009–present), and Donald Trump on *The Apprentice* retain their classed New York or North Jersey accents. These sounds become ghosts of a city and register moments in urban history when intimacy between classes existed through shared social spaces and dreams of economic mobility. When we hear Jill Zarin talk, she speaks New York's past. When she says her husband's name, Bobby Zarin, it sounds like "Baweby Zayrihn." When Jill says the word *offer*, it sounds like "awe-fur." Likewise, Newman argues that Donald Trump speaks with a New York City accent; *The Apprentice* and *Celebrity Apprentice* showcase his accent. Although Trump's speech is not marked strictly working class, the way he pronounces his vowels and drops his h are indicative of a non-elite way of speaking emerging from Queens, where Trump grew up.[12] The New York City accent in the Trump family has gone through three phases: Donald's father, who grew up working class and retained that speech pattern, even though he became wealthy; Donald, who still holds many speech patterns from this dialect; and Trump's children who are a third-generation moneyed class who no longer have a New York City accent.

Urban reality programs and the publicity machines around them contain moments that place these sounds within classed geographies. A noticeable dialect difference exists between Bethenny and Jill and the Van Kempens on *The Real Housewives of New York* City. Simon, an Australian hotel mogul, and his wife, Alex, who comes from Texas oil money, speak proper English. After Season One, Simon makes a comment to the press about how Jill sounds like a trashy Long Islander. The opening few episodes of Season Two deal with the controversy stemming from that. Likewise, Bethenny Frankel, who would eventually build her Skinny Girl brand empire and become incredibly rich, begins Season One with the only modest apartment of the cast. It's a cramped space that looks like a tiny student rental in most college towns, even though its Upper East Side location puts it out of the range of most professionals. Bethenny is coded as beneath the status of the other women at first, and her accent connects her to her status. While all of the other women own summer homes in the Hamptons, Bethenny is forced to stay with Jill and Bobby there as she is trying to start her brand.

Like the accents we hear, the plots and premises of urban reality programs summon older assumptions about urban life and intimacy. One of the most common premises on reality television is for a program to follow a family business. Some businesses on reality television pride themselves on being multigenerational and rooted in a history that dates back to the industrial era. On MTV's *The Osbornes* (2002–05), Sharon Osborne, and her father before her, had managed her rock star husband Ozzy since the early 1970s. On *The Real Housewives of New York*, Jill has married into the Zarin family that has operated its own fabric store in Greenwich Village since 1936. On the same show, Ramona married into the Singer family that has been running True Faith Jewelry for three generations. NBC's *The Apprentice* features Donald Trump and his children teaching upstart business people and celebrities how to be as successful as his family. Patti Stanger on Bravo's *The Millionaire Matchmaker* (2008–15) finds people the perfect romantic partner because she is a third-generation matchmaker. Tia Maria Torres runs her nonprofit pitbull rescue with her four children and their partners on Animal Planet's *Pitbulls and Parolees*. People on other reality television shows are first-generation family business owners. On Bravo's *Flipping Out*, professional house flipper Jeff Lewis becomes business partners with his boyfriend Gage Edwards, and the two look to find a surrogate mother and become fathers on the show. TLC's *Cake Boss* follows Buddy Valastro and his siblings who own a family-run cake business in Hoboken, New Jersey.

Reality television's presentation of the city as a site of family business nostalgically looks to periods of older industrialisms in American history. Economic historian Andrea Colli argues that, although family businesses still exist in the age of post-industrial global capitalism, they are a carryover from an early period of industrialization when labor relations, communication networks, and markets were small and regional. These are the firms that started industry in the nineteenth century and that typically appear in newly industrialized countries.[13] Although the previous chapter talked about the openness of post-World War II urban spaces, it is important to note here that the same large-scale industries that were part of an economy that fairly distributed wealth were often viewed as impersonal and anti-individualistic. Arthur Miller's *Death of a Salesman* and Rod Serling's *Patterns* explore how corporations tossed employees aside when they no longer served their functions. In *White Collar*, C. Wright Mills talked about corporations robbing people of their identities. William Whyte, Jr., wrote about *The Organization Man*, a figure constructed to say yes to authority. Much of these fears stem from the lack of intimacy in managerial corporations. As Colli argues, the growth of industrialization required the separation of ownership from management. This is a vertical structure of authority where workers fail to create close relationships with those in power because large-scale production requires atomized control. The family business contrasts with this by operating through a flat structure. Owners and bosses are the same; employees work closely with them. Decisions are often less hierarchical, as the family becomes involved in business matters.[14] This structure welcomes the imagination that Mills and Whyte found lacking in corporations, for the family business flourishes in light-scale industries that rely on creativity more than capital-intensive industries do. As a result, sensibilities and competencies formed between family members and employees flourish here. Although advanced phases of industrialism required large-scale manufacturing and then global financing, the family business, in decline throughout the decades, survives because this older way of business fills niches.[15]

This larger economic history of the family business shapes the way reality television uses the trope to show familial intimacy, generosity, and love. On *Pitbulls and Parolees*, the plot with reformed drug addict and parolee Perry in Season Five shows the closeness of the work environment. As Perry overcomes his addictions while working at Villalobos, he starts to date Tia's daughter Tonia. His ability to be a good person is shown to be directly linked to his ability to cultivate a romance. As Perry blossoms as an ideal employee, he marries Tonia and becomes a member of the family running Villalobos. The marriage episode shows how Tia, as a boss, has an intimacy with her work and family. Tonia and Perry's wedding is about to take place when a tropical storm hits New Orleans. The storm requires extra preparation to insure the rescue center located in the flood-susceptible lower ninth ward is safe. While Tonia plans to cancel the wedding to help secure the warehouse and possibly move the pitbulls to another location, Tia helps her focus on her wedding to find familial bliss. Tia takes on extra responsibilities at the shelter, talks Tonia through prewedding jitters, and even attends the wedding after her shelter dogs are safe.

Even when romance isn't involved at Villalobos, the compassionate nature of the care at the animal shelter spills into sympathies outside of work and expands the intimate nature of being in a family. For example, Tia unofficially adopted two Hawaiian twins, Kanani and Moe, after her daughter Maria met the two troubled boys at school. Tia hires them at Villalobos and refers to them as her children. Also, one of the parolees, Earl, suffered an injury in prison that left his right arm paralyzed. Tia's family makes special efforts so Earl can live comfortably with his disability. Tia's daughter Maria knits Earl a sling, and the Torres family helps Earl find a clinic for people without insurance. Two seasons later, Earl travels to a doctor in Florida for a successful surgery on his herniated disc, and Tia comments that Earl deserves the best because she considers him a family member.

Another intimacy of *Pitbulls and Parolees* occurs through Tia's ability to work closely with marginalized people in a way that exposes the audience to flaws in the justice system. This is evident when she hires ex-Tulane football star Tony Converse, a working-class kid from New Orleans who went to prison for eleven years for selling marijuana. When Tony applies for a job at Villalobos, Tia swells up with tears when she hears of the way a judge punished Tony for a nonviolent crime. The next several episodes show Tia working with Tony at the shelter and on rescues. She says in many confessionals that Tony is a hard worker, a great addition to the Villalobos family, and a good person. The closeness of Tia's business offers a benevolence missing from the impersonal nature of the justice system.

The family business also creates an intimate bond between the cast members, the viewers, and the American dream of class mobility. Often episodes within these series include memories of class mobility, but not of the family members who started the business. Focus is on the people who married into the family and rose in class because of that. In *The Real Housewives of New York City*, Jill sometimes reflects on growing up as a middle-class Jew on Long Island and how she married into the wealthy Zarin family. Similarly, Ramona discusses her days studying to be a fashion designer at the Fashion Institute of Design and Marketing in New York City and how meeting and marrying Mario Singer helped her become rich. MTV's *The Osbornes* includes discussions about how Ozzy was a working-class kid from Birmingham who became a rock star in part through the smart management of his wife's father. If downward social mobility is the typical movement people experience in the age of social expulsions, reality television programs recall historical moments of upward class mobility, only marriage replaces hard work as a way to achieve the American dream.

The family business on urban reality shows also creates intimate economic markets by shrinking them from a global to a local scale, helping to define the city and its region as bounded within a specific space constituted by the closeness of classes. It's common on *The Apprentice* and later on *The Celebrity Apprentice* for Donald Trump to have his contestants do fundraisers and business campaigns for local New York City businesses. When Geraldo Rivera led his team of celebrities to write a jingle for the coffee company Chock Full o' Nuts, he says he grew up in New York City in a working-class section of the Bronx drinking this coffee and listening to its jingles play on local radio stations. Perhaps the most comical portrait of the family business grounding economics in localized markets and class intimacies comes in an episode of *Wahlburgers* (2014–present), the A & E reality show about the restaurant owned and operated by the celebrity family the Wahlbergs. Actors and singers Mark and Donnie opened a restaurant in Hingham, Massachusetts, with their brother Paul, who is a chef. The show presents a close-knit family marked as working class through their accents and friendships, even though Mark and Donnie have successful careers as entertainers. In one episode, family friends Johnny "Drama" Alves and Henry "Nacho" Laun fly from Massachusetts to Los Angeles to visit Mark, who is living at his LA home during a movie shoot. Mark requests that his friends bring him a dozen burgers from his family restaurant because nothing tastes as good in Los Angeles. Here the family is bound within the Boston region that offers different tastes and cultures than Los Angeles. The laugh of the episode comes when the family's obese and clownish friend Nacho eats all twelve burgers on the flight from Boston to Los Angeles, an act of gluttony that allows Mark to experience home through the childish behavior of his working-class buddy. Bloated and having a hard time breathing, Nacho proceeds to hit golf balls with Mark and Johnny from Mark's backyard into the neighborhood, a juvenile act of criminality that also codes the three men as working-class Bostonians who can't fit in with the new class etiquette of Beverly Hills.

One of the crucial intimacies on these shows is that family business owners work closely with clients, who often aren't coded as rich residents of exclusive cities but appear to be just like every other viewer. The Real Housewives of New York City frequently shows Jill working at Zarin Fabrics. Random customers come in looking for items such as new blinds. One pair of clients are billed as gay guys from Queens; their job titles are never given to reveal their true economic status. While Queens has many neighborhoods that are gentrified, coding the clients as Queens' residents positions them as part of a historical constituent of working-class residents of that borough.

Additionally, family businesses are coded as working so closely with clients that they, in fact, have a better knowledge of the clients than the clients actually do. This functions as part of the comical premise of The Millionaire Matchmaker (2008–15). Patti Stanger will interview a millionaire looking for a partner and figure out why this person has failed at love. As a third-generation matchmaker, Patti interviews dozens of potential partners for her client and chooses two types of people: (1) those who would be ideal matches; and (2) one person who is the same type of person the client has picked in the past (not a good match). Patti brings all of these people together at a mixer and monitors her client's interaction with them until the client picks two people with whom to go on an individual date. Throughout this process, Patti comments on how the client is learning to make the right romantic choices, or she will comically belittle the client for falling into bad habits.

Even when programs about local family businesses don't seem to be about class intimacies within regional markets, class can function in complex ways where fluidity marks intimacy. Here one person experiences class intimacies through his or her own unstable relationship to class structures. Take *Flipping Out*, a show about real-estate flipper Jeff Lewis. Ostensibly the series is about Jeff working with wealthy clients in Los Angeles. Jeff himself appears as a member of this social class. He dresses in expensive clothes and drives luxury cars. But Jeff's class status isn't set. The series started at the height of the real-estate bubble when Jeff could purchase run-down houses for a low price and flip them for premium market value. But during the recession, Jeff's class status became very fragile. No longer able to sell flipped houses in an aggressive market, he had to take on less glamorous jobs such as interior decorator in order to pay bills. Later seasons capture Jeff's triumphant return to the flip business, but the series has coded him variously as someone ranging from a middle-class decorator for hire to a real-estate tycoon. Thus, even a family business show that seems to be just about the rich actually offers a heterotopic view of class relations.

Something similar happens on Bravo's *The Millionaire Matchmaker*. Although matchmaker Patti Stanger dresses in expensive designer clothes and drives luxury cars, she retains a working-class New Jersey accent from her childhood. Her behavior when talking with clients is lowbrow. As Pierre Bourdieu tells us, taste cultures often break down along class lines, as lowly tastes often are the result of bodily pleasures associated with the lower class, whose lack of access to educational advancement insures labor and leisure associated with the body.[16] When Patti coaches her millionaire clients on how to act on dates, her crude gestures incite viewers to recoil in disgust. It's common for her to point to her various body parts as she tells her clients to avoid sexual activity on the date: "I don't want to hear about you putting it in here [mouth], here [vagina], or here [anus]." Thus, while Patti moves through exclusive areas of Los Angeles, her conflicting class codes make this a place of upper-class people and lower-class cultures.

In addition to the family business, the level playing field premise summons older periods of industrial social relations amidst contemporary global capitalist cities. The term level playing field comes from sporting cultures and suggests that social inequalities of race, class, gender, region, nation, and other identity categories do not matter in athletic competitions. Ability, individual will, and preparation—not systems of socioeconomic privilege and oppression—determine success. CBS's The Amazing Race is a competition where teams of two race around the world and compete against each other in challenges typically set in global cities; the show's producers consistently cast teams from various racial, gendered, and class backgrounds to draw upon the athletic discourse of the level playing field.

The Amazing Race nostalgically envisions city spaces as places where all social classes exist and can thrive through their determination to win. Season Seven brings these class dynamics into focus; the final four are marked as working-, middle-, and upper-class Americans. The eventual winners, Uchenna and Joyce, are two African American corporate executives from Houston who lost their jobs because of the Enron and WorldCom scandals. Meredith and Gretchen are two senior citizens who married later in life. Meredith is a retired executive and has money, but Gretchen is a former flight attendant and nurse. Survivor contestants Boston Rob Mariano and his wife, Amber, also competed on this season. Although Amber won the All-Stars season of Survivor and got the million dollars, Boston Rob has a thick working-class Bostonian accent and is always billed as a construction worker. Likewise, Ron and Kelly appear to be southern working class, as Ron speaks with a heavy southern accent and is an ex-soldier who has gone back to school. His girlfriend, Kelly, is a legislative correspondent. While African Americans, the elderly, and the working class have historically faced hardships within the American imaginary, the level playing field on The Amazing Race creates space where each group, and each social class, can compete to be the best. The final two teams in the race were a delight to watch. Uchenna and Joyce showed their class status through their refined accents and proper upper-class behavior, while Boston Rob came across as a slick working-class urban con who encouraged travel agents to give other teams bad flights and made deals with locals so they would help him and not the other competitors.

On *The Amazing Race*, the line demarcating the field of play from the rest of society is blurred, to the point of being almost illegible. The field in sports is built into a space separate from the flow of society. The field is closed off to through traffic and, in the case of professional sports, only open during game time. Thus, sports become a vehicle through which people can remove themselves from oppressive structures through a space that exists apart from society. But in *The Amazing Race*, cities around the globe are the playing fields. Competitions are set in the hearts of cities and involve teams racing through streets and partaking in challenges as normal life continues in a city. In fact, the city is so much a part of the level playing field that rush hours and traffic congestion affect the teams' success. Often a team's placement in a leg of the race is determined by their cab driver's knowledge of city routes. When the race starts and finishes in American cities such as Los Angeles, Miami, or Dallas, it appears as if all classes inhabit these spaces and have a chance to be upwardly mobile. Any couple can make it on *The Amazing Race*, as long as they minimize fighting and try hard.

Figure 2.1 *The Amazing Race* host Phil Keoghan poses with two racers at a pit stop in San Francisco. The city functions as part of the playing field.

CBS/Photofest ©CBS

Many sites of competitions on *The Amazing Race* are global capitalist cities that make up a larger political economy of expulsions. These cities that have been redefined as business, residential, and leisure zones for the elite become the sites where people on the program can fight for upward mobility. Paris, Amsterdam, Berlin, Vienna, London, Tokyo, San Paulo, Buenos Aires, and Rio de Janeiro have all appeared on the program. The competitions set within cities buttress the program's vision of industrial class egalitarianism by presenting the city as a space grounded in historical traditions, not contemporary economies. A detour competition (where the teams choose one of two challenges) set in Krakow, Poland, in Season Twenty-seven gives contestants the option to move salt through one of the city's salt mines or to move a piano through the streets and play a simple tune for money in a park. The first option highlights the city's history as a major mineral producer, and the second one instructs viewers about the city's distinguished musical history. In Season Twenty-six, one of the detour options in Tokyo asks contestants to memorize the names of ten bottles of saké and then take the saké orders of numerous samurai at the Nakano Sakaue Station Tavern. Later that season, teams travel to Munich, Germany, and dress in traditional work clothes (lederhosen for men and dirndl for women). In Season Nineteen, teams also dress in a period costume in Copenhagen, Denmark, in order to learn a historical dance routine. Thus, even the classes that people perform in actual competitions in *The Amazing Race* create a class intimacy, as contestants have to perform former identities rooted in various socioeconomic classes, ranging all the way from Germany's manual laborers to Poland's elite musicians. Class intimacy on this program registers both through the interactions of various classes in the cities and through the performance of various classes by the contestants.

Another premise of reality television that presents the city in nostalgic terms is successful entrepreneurship. This might come as a shock to readers familiar with the importance of the concept of entrepreneurship in media studies writings about neoliberalism. These significant works contend that, as the economy has been deregulated and state programs have been cut, responsibility and risk are transferred to the individual. Alice Marwick argues that self-entrepreneurship and self-branding become a hallmark of twenty-first-century citizenship. Within this body of literature, entrepreneurship equates with risk taking and risk management.[17] The term *entrepreneur* has a long history, though, and an examination of its history as an idea reveals that its nineteenth- and twentieth-century meanings often position it against the figure of the capitalist and view it as a means to change the current economic order. These histories shape the portrait of entrepreneurs on reality television, who function as imaginative citizens that correct the brutality and exclusivity of the contemporary economy. Through their spatial freedom within cities and with their ability to represent dated assumptions about the American dream and class mobility, the entrepreneur opens space.

According to economic historians Robert F. Hebert and Albert N. Link, the intellectual history of the term *entrepreneur* in America pitted the figure against the capitalist through the tensions between disequilibrium and equilibrium as well as uncertainty and risk. Going back to the idea of the entrepreneur in economic theory reveals an American imaginary where the entrepreneur uses sentiments of American individualism to define him or herself as distinct from contemporary economic trends. Legendary theorist of entrepreneurship Joseph Schumpeter argues that economies operate through flows whereby capitalists hold onto practices that maintain the status quo or equilibrium. The entrepreneur, however, disturbs this flow and functions as a mechanism for economic change. Schumpeter calls this process "creative destruction." He also claims that the capitalist, as an owner of goods, takes on risk for money, profit, and goods that could be lost in business transactions. The entrepreneur, on the contrary, manages uncertainty. The entrepreneur is not an owner of goods and thus risks little. Rather, amazing abilities to innovate allow the entrepreneur to make new combinations in production that could potentially repackage items that cost less to buy and more to sell. This innovative redirection of capital included creating new products or a new quality within existing products, creating new production methods, unlocking markets, finding a new supply source, and creating a new method of production. Although economists in the nineteenth and early twentieth century disagreed on what exactly differentiated the capitalist from the entrepreneur, nearly all theorists, including Amasa Walker, Francis Walker, Frederick Hawley, John Bates Clark, Hebert Davenport, Frank Taussig, and Frank Knight, distinguished these two figures.[18]

Many economic theories of entrepreneurship portrayed this economic actor through tropes of individualism that deeply resonated with myths of individualism and the American dream. Schumpeter labelled the entrepreneur a "supernormal economic agent" because of his or her ability to read markets well and to work innovatively. Max Weber, whose work on entrepreneurship influenced many American economists, argued the entrepreneur succeeded because of a Protestant commitment to hard work. Both views resonate with American national identity, as Schumpeter drew on a discourse of exceptionalism interwoven with our views of nationhood. Weber made entrepreneurship available to more people, as his views aligned with American notions of hard work leading to economic success and class mobility. In fact, Schumpeter argued that entrepreneurs are not a social class, which helped to define this business group as individuals capable of climbing class hierarchies.[19]

Writings on entrepreneurship often use spatial metaphors to convey freedom and mobility. Schumpeter envisioned the entrepreneur as a newcomer who swims against the tide. Spatially, this moves the status quo in one direction, a direction that has considerable force and is hard to stop. But the entrepreneur has the freedom and power to move in a different direction. Individualism is spatialized in a straight line here. In another passage, Schumpeter talked about the entrepreneur as someone who breaks away from the pack, again positioning the entrepreneur in different movement through space than capitalists.[20] Post-World War II sociologist C. Wright Mills argued that the new breed of entrepreneurs in the postwar era found autonomy and creativity by moving between business institutions. For Mills, dependent employees worked within one industry and functioned as corporate yes men who simply took orders from above. Space was a top-down form of vertical power. But the entrepreneur moved horizontally. Between industries, the entrepreneur found ways to work with imagination and avoid any control that robbed him or her of individuality.[21] Winner of the 2006 Nobel Prize in Economic Science, Edmund S. Phelps wrote an article for the *Wall Street Journal* in that same year titled "Dynamic Capitalism" where he contrasted entrepreneurial economies and corporate economies. Phelps praised the former for providing "openness, encouragement, and flexibility."[22] The first of the descriptive words, *openness*, describes the economy in terms of space and uses the same terminology as

Doreen Massey does in her writings on place. For a space to be open, it must make relationships malleable and changeable. Opening space for entrepreneurship implies that the status quo can be changed so that people can find new forms of dignity and humanity in a space.

These points become important for the representation of entrepreneurship on reality television, for the figure often casts city spaces through nostalgia. If contemporary American cities have become closed spaces serving as nodal points in a network of global capitalism, reality television entrepreneurs transform these cities into open spaces where American dreams occur. In this way, realty TV entrepreneurs put one of the foundational purposes of entrepreneurship into action: the ability to cause economic disequilibrium. These entrepreneurs wrest the city away from financing and return it to the people. Their ability to achieve class mobility is mirrored in their own movements within cities themselves.

Bravo's Bethenny Frankel is a fascinating case in point. Frankel began her tenure on Bravo during the first season of *The Real Housewives of New York City*, but she brought with her a different classed identity than the other housewives did. Although all of the housewives would dabble in entrepreneurial adventures on this series, Frankel was the only one who was completely reliant on her entrepreneurial success for her financial wellness. The other women came from family money, so when Alex McCord and Jill Zarin wrote books, they did so to earn more money for their elite bank accounts. When Luann de Lesseps recorded a techno song, she did so to promote her brand, but her divorce settlement from a European royal family member insured she would maintain her level of wealth. Bethenny, however, needed her entrepreneurship in order to enter the world of New York's elite class.

Bethenny's relationship to her family codes her as a class outsider on *The Real Housewives*. Whereas Alex McCord comes from a wealthy Texas oil family and Jill, Ramona, and Luann married into wealthy families, Bethenny both comes from a broken home and had not yet married when the show premiered. Her own family's financial status was a bit nebulous. Bethenny spent her early years at the race track. Her father owned race horses, a profession that requires serious cash investments. Yet Bethenny separated from her abusive family and claimed she had to rely on herself for economic support, making it seem like she chose to start life on her own in rags. Her first reality television show appearance was on NBC's *The Apprentice: Martha Stewart* (2005), where Bethenny made it to the final two, distinguishing herself as a tough New York ethnic Jew who foiled the calm, waspy winner, Dawna Stone. Bethenny's initial charm on the show was that she wasn't perfect like Stone. She got stressed. She mouthed off. She had temper tantrums. In short, Bethenny acted like many of us would in a similar situation.

Figure 2.2 Bethenny Frankel and her more down-to-earth yet still elegant image.
Fox Television Network/Photofest ©Fox Television Network

Bethenny's Jewishness serves as a classed form of authenticity on *The Real Housewives*, as her neurotic humor could pick apart everyday mannerisms a la Jerry Seinfeld and Larry David to show the realness behind the pretentious lives of the rich. Perhaps the best example of this comes when she and Luann take a limousine from Luann's Upper East Side townhome to a downtown restaurant. Bethenny introduces her friend to the limousine driver as Luann, and Luann immediately chastises her for not using her proper name, "The Countess de Lesseps." During the car ride to the restaurant, the episode cuts in hilarious confessionals of Bethenny commenting on Luann's demand. Bethenny notes that Luann isn't even royalty. She's a woman from Connecticut who married a count. She also wonders why a random limo driver would need to know she is a countess and even goes as far as to bring up Luann's former occupation as a nurse to suggest that she and the limo driver share a class status. Bethenny's common-sense approach to wealth also gives a humorous window to the truth when Jill brings Bethenny to her Upper East Side apartment to show Bethenny her multi-million-dollar apartment renovation. While the other women have been wowed by Jill's spectacle of wealth, Bethenny claims that the apartment "looks like Liberace threw up in it." Here Bethenny is able to see past wealth as a spectacle and evaluate the renovation from the perspective of modest good taste.

As an entrepreneur, Bethenny is able to package her no-frills, common-sense proletariat approach to life in her Skinny Girl brand. Bethenny created a series of mixed drinks, wines, and cookbooks. The hallmark of her brand is that people can live a healthy lifestyle and not give up on taste as long as they consume modestly. Thus, as an entrepreneur, Bethenny sells the very point of view she delivers on the Bravo series: she offers people a real and achievable lifestyle as long as they don't overindulge.

Bethenny's success as an entrepreneur occurs through her own relationship to city spaces. Her successful launch and development of the Skinny Girl brand take her from a single woman living in a cramped Manhattan apartment to her luxurious downtown condo where she lives with her husband, Jason. Unlike the other women on the show, Bethenny is the main provider in her family's monetary success, as Jason earns a mere $100,000 a year, which is relatively low for the per capita average in Manhattan. Her success is measured by her ability to move up in social status and into new classed spaces. However, Bethenny retains her connections to spaces for the people. Bethenny often does publicity appearances for her books in book stores for middle-class people and addresses a working audience. Moreover, in an episode of Bethenny Ever After (2010–12), she does a book signing at on outer borough Costco, a discount wholesale food store, and then proceeds to grocery shop at the store after the signing, a move that presents her as still one of us. Thus, Bethenny accesses a range of classed spaces in the city, as she is coded as an upwardly mobile success and as still one of the 99 percent. This specific combination of class signs makes it appear as if the city is accommodating of this range of class positions and that the city still affords those in the working and middle classes the opportunity to work hard and improve their economic status.

Bethenny Frankel embodies the long history of entrepreneurship's ability to bring a disequilibrium to the economy, for she frustrates the series' portrait of wealth belonging to established money and the 1 percent. Bethenny is so relatable to viewers because she stands for old tropes of economic success in city spaces that no longer allow it. Whereas the other women on the series have a right to be in these exclusive spaces through their well-established family wealth, Bethenny must risk her brand and her own position in this society in order to grow her business and accumulate enough money to move up the social scale within New York's wealth. That she manages to do this while maintaining her connection to working- and middle-class spaces shows that the entrepreneur does not simply belong with the elite. The entrepreneur fights and climbs to join this circle.

CONCLUSION

This chapter has offered a broad overview of the way that visuals, sound, and plots come together on twenty-first-century urban reality shows to win our consent for the political economy of social expulsions. Reality television offers a reflective nostalgia that is part of a diasporic imagination that sees past homes sprinkled throughout present spaces. Visually, reality television presents us with spaces of contemporary closed cities. Shot distance and editing make us enjoy the city from afar. We see sanitized images of the city that rob it of any dynamic interaction between social groups, and the splicing together of space edits out poverty to preserve the image of luxury. This is not the home that various classed residents knew during the industrial era. Yet reality television makes us long for that era through the classed voices we hear and through the stories of industrial capitalism that we follow. The sound and plots of the city are ghosts of another era, one where all classes lived in the city, that haunt the closed spaces of contemporary cities and allow us to see bits and pieces of our former homes. We come to accept the closed spaces of the city on these shows because it seems like urban space still can function as a home to all social classes. Although this chapter has explored how the city appeals to classes who can no longer afford to live there, the next chapter examines how Bravo reality television programs win our consent for urban social expulsions through the way that othered servants and servers normalize the rich and redeem the political economy.

NOTES

1 Zygmunt Bauman, Community: Seeking Safety in an Insecure World (Malden, MA: Polity, 2001).
2 John Durham Peters, "Nomadism, Diaspora, Exile: The Stakes of Mobility with the Western Canon," in Hamid Nacify, ed., Home, Exile, Homeland: Film, Media, and the Politics of Place (New York: Routledge, 1999), 17–44.
3 Svetlana Boym, The Future of Nostalgia (New York: Basic Books, 2002), 251–3.
4 Michael Dwyer, Back to the Fifties: Nostalgia, Hollywood Film, and Popular Music of the Seventies and Eighties (New York: Oxford University Press, 2015), 4.
5 Svetlana Boym, The Future of Nostalgia (New York: Basic Books, 2002), 41–55.
6 John Thornton Caldwell, Televisuality: Style, Crisis, and Authority in American Television (New Brunswick, NJ: Rutgers University Press, 1995); Jeremy Butler, Television Style, 1st edition (New York, Routledge: 2009); Brett Mills, "What Does It Mean to Call Television 'Cinematic'?" in Jason Jacobs and Steven Peacock, eds, Television Aesthetics and Style (New York: Bloomsbury, 2013), 57–66.
7 Laura Mulvey, Visual and Other Pleasures (Bloomington, IN: Indiana University Press, 1989), 14–28; Thomas Gunning, "The Cinema of Attraction[s]: Early Film, Its Spectators and the Avant Garde," in Wanda Strauven, ed., The Cinema of Attractions Reloaded (Amsterdam: University of Amsterdam Press, 2007), 381–8.
8 Richard Dyer, Only Entertainment, 2nd edition (New York: Routledge, 2002), 28–30.

9 Svetlana Boym, *The Future of Nostalgia* (New York: Basic Books, 2002), 251–3.

10 Michael Newman, *New York City English* (Berlin: De Gruyter Mouton, 2014), 1–24.

11 Hansi Lo Wang, "Fuhgeddaboudit: New York Accent on its Way Out, Linguists Say," NPR.org, February 2, 2015. Accessed December 10, 2015. http://www.npr.org/2015/02/02/383289958/fuhgeddaboudit-new-york-accent-on-its-way-out-linguists-say.

12 Magee Hickey, "Who Has the Better New York Accent: Sanders or Trump?" Pix11.com, February 19, 2016. Accessed July 11, 2016. http://pix11.com/2016/02/19/who-has-the-better-new-york-accent-sanders-or-trump/.

13 Andrea Colli, *The History of Family Business, 1850–2000* (New York: Cambridge University Press, 2003), 8–11, 28–30.

14 Andrea Colli, *The History of Family Business, 1850–2000* (New York: Cambridge University Press, 2003), 49–72.

15 Andrea Colli, *The History of Family Business, 1850–2000* (New York: Cambridge University Press, 2003), 74.

16 Pierre Bourdieu, *Distinctions: A Social Critique of the Judgement of Taste* (Cambridge, MA: Harvard University Press, 1984).

17 Alice Marwick, *Status Update: Celebrity, Publicity, and Branding in the Social Media Age* (New Haven, CT: Yale University Press, 2015).

18 Robert F. Hebert and Albert N. Link, *A History of Entrepreneurship* (New York: Routledge, 2009), 55–77.

19 Robert F. Hebert and Albert N. Link, *A History of Entrepreneurship* (New York: Routledge, 2009), 67–77.

20 Robert F. Hebert and Albert N. Link, *A History of Entrepreneurship* (New York: Routledge, 2009), 67–77.

21 C. Wright Mills, *White Collar: The American Middle Classes* (New York: Oxford University Press, 1951).

22 Robert F. Hebert and Albert N. Link, *A History of Entrepreneurship* (New York: Routledge, 2009), vii.

3

BRAVO AND THE GEOGRAPHIES
OF URBAN SERVITUDE

Servants and servers are crucial to the operations of contemporary global cities. They take care of the homes, children, and pets of the rich so that those wealthy business people can focus on their work. They also work in metropolitan restaurants and leisure industries for the elite residents. They perform janitorial and maid services within buildings of global finances. Despite this, servants and servers remain noticeably absent from most twenty-first-century urban reality programs. Certainly, real servants work on the sets of urban reality shows, but programs keep this class off screen. Moreover, reality programs rarely focus exclusively on a community of servers. Telling these stories would visualize the way that urban prosperity is buttressed by economic abjection. The televisual invisibility of servants and servers mirrors the logic of New York City's poor doors—separate entrances for the poor in newly built New York City residential buildings—by which the economically downtrodden remain close but are kept at bay.

Bravo is the only cable station that, on a consistent basis, metaphorically opens its poor doors to televise the lives of servants and servers. Sometimes, as is the case with *The Real Housewives of Beverly Hills* (2010–present), the servants merely exist in the background, as they are shown setting up for and working at elite social events. But servants also appear as developed characters on the shows. *The Real Housewives of New York City's* (2008–present) Rosie is Luann de Lesseps' housekeeper and, at times, stand-in mom, as the Countess needs someone regularly to take care of her children while she attends social functions, dates men after her divorce, and begins her career as a recording artist. *Flipping Out* (2007–present) dedicates time to real-estate flipper Jeff Lewis' housekeeper, Zoila; she often provides comic relief to tensions in Jeff's office. *Vanderpump Rules* (2013–present) offers the most extended look at the lives of servers. It focuses entirely on the servers who work at the restaurant Sur, which is owned and operated by *The Real Housewives of Beverly Hills* cast member Lisa Vanderpump.

Analyzing the geographic significance of servants and servers on these shows requires an inquiry into Bravo's brand. Television scholars point out that, as the era of broadcasting came to an end in the early 1980s, creating a brand became an important part of running a successful cable station. Joseph Turow claims the brand is the core identity of a channel that makes it stand out as unique amidst many competing options.[1] Catherine Johnson argues that the brand identity of a channel creates expectations of its programming for its viewers, noting that "brands are thus frames of action that manage the relationship around branded products and services."[2] As Amanda Ann Klein and Erin Copple Smith show, cable channels often create brands that attract an audience by packing identities in programs for commercial and political purposes.[3] This leads to two central questions for the chapter: (1) why does Bravo package the identity of servants and servers in order to further its brand image and cater to the desires executives envision in their audience; and (2) how does this help to win our consent for the political economy of social expulsions?

Bravo represents servants and servers on its reality programs not to sympathize with them but to applaud the closed spaces of the political economy of expulsions and the elite's position within them. Bravo's identity is partly based on the celebration of affluence, a strategy that assures that programs about society's elite help attract a wealthy, young, hip urban audience. At the same time, Bravo prizes irony that mocks hypocritical wealthy cast members. These two branding initiatives create a contradictory viewing position for viewers whereby characters are held up as models of wealth and objects of scorn. Nevertheless, the urban geographies of expulsion on Bravo remain aspirational and celebratory, requiring that the programs find ways to redeem wealth for the channel's viewers.

Bravo reality programs stabilize a positive reading of geographies of affluence by showing their superiority to geographies of servitude. The power relationship between these two economic areas surfaces through the way that servants and servers are "othered." Broadly speaking, to other a social group is to construct them as different through stigmas and fears. Othering upholds dominant cultural norms through its inability to understand difference in its own terms. Othering justifies domination and control of a subordinate social group, for it sees this group as lacking qualities crucial to a narrowly defined view of humanity created by those with social power. Othering the economically vulnerable on Bravo programs allows the rich to be seen as the norm, even if the norm is something we occasionally laugh at and deride. The normalizing process of the rich helps to win our consent for the political economy of social expulsions, as our framework for what constitutes a good society becomes centered on this socioeconomic group.

Bravo programming others servants and servers by portraying them as failures or incomplete humans whose own shortcomings highlight the successful citizenship and business practices of their wealthy employers. The shows place servants and servers in spatial relationships where their spaces of moral corruption need to be policed by ethically superior elites, where their servitude allows them to exist as noble savages who are part of the natural beauty of the wealthy estates, and where their racial identities become justification either to expel them from or to entrap them in the home. This positions elite areas in the political economy of expulsions as desirable for viewers, for these spaces either correct the flaws of service industry workers or allow servants to find completion through their domestic labor. Othering servants and servers allows the rich to emerge as benevolent helpers of the poor and wins our consent for the political economy by deceptively convincing viewers that the closed urban spaces in the era of social expulsions are normal, not brutal.

CONTRADICTORY IDEAS OF WEALTH IN BRAVO'S BRAND

Cable channel brands frequently lack absolute coherence. As the field of media industry studies shows us, television executives engage in struggles shaped by uneven power relationships to create both a television brand and a programming lineup. While companies are hierarchical and follow executive decisions on branding, areas of contradiction within the brand surface for many reasons. Sometimes executives working concurrently create different branding initiatives that frame some programs and not others. Other times, new executives join a station and maintain old branding strategies while starting others. Bravo's brand came about because different executives created different viewing strategies. One-time president Rachel Zalaznick started the notion of the affluencer, Bravo's ideal wealthy viewer who found her or his mirror in Bravo programs, to sell advertising space to upscale companies. However, Bravo head of programming development and television producer Andy Cohen developed reality shows that mocked wealthy contestants. This made Bravo programming both a mirror to reflect viewers and a microscope to see the unpleasant nature of a different breed of humans.

Erin Copple Smith details how Bravo's intended viewers see themselves on Bravo programming. Bravo's audience is made up of women and gay men who are educated, upscale (25 percent make over $100,000 a year), and live in metropolitan areas. Zalaznak focuses less on demographics than on psychographics, which essentializes the audience to a few identity traits. The profile of Bravo's affluencer is someone whose income power matches her or his cultural influence. This audience has the money to purchase cutting-edge trends. A magazine titled Bravo Affluencer, distributed to potential advertisers for the channel, described the audience as "attractive men and women, both in their late 20s, shopping bags and PDA (personal digital assistants) in hand, passports visible in pockets, dressed casually but stylishly, plugged in on top of that."[4] Copple Smith propounds that Bravo's programming strategy "has been to display these prototypical affluencers within the channel's series in an effort to reinforce this particular construction of the audience."[5] For example, Flipping Out's Jeff Lewis, a gay male in his thirties who lives in Los Angeles and is constantly using his mobile phone and Mac laptop, is a trend-setting real-estate developer. Likewise, Patti Stanger, on The Millionaire Matchmaker, is both an affluencer living in LA and head of a dating service for affluencers in the city.

Michael J. Lee and Leigh Moscowitz unearth a different aspect of Bravo's brand: irony, a trait that often shows affluencers at their worst. According to the authors, the following quote from Bravo's Andy Cohen is telling:

> We do something with the editing that is called the Bravo wink. We
> wink at the audience when someone says "I'm the healthiest person in
> the world" and then you see them ashing their cigarette. We are kind
> of letting our audience in on the fun.[6]

Bravo's employment of irony presents their wealthy characters as objects of
derision. For the authors, irony gains its powers from what is not said. It opens
up room for alternative and contradictory interpretations from the audience
because the opposite of what is onscreen is meant. Lee and Moscowitz argue
that Bravo programs such as *The Real Housewives of New York City* feature wealthy
women, only to tear them apart through irony to reveal how money corrupts
their abilities to be good women, mothers, and friends. Bravo upholds the
figure of the "rich bitch," a trope that derides women of affluence through
normative assumptions of class and gender. Such ironic constructions of
meaning are possible because the affluencer audience for Bravo is known for
its cultural capital and being well versed in complicated reading strategies.[7]

But what is the norm on Bravo? Lee and Moscowitz are right when they
claim that the mocking of the rich bitch on the programs occurs through a
lens that sees the world through a more middle-class view, but that relationship between an assumed middle-class spectator and a wealthy cast member
is only one class relationship on Bravo. Just as important is the onscreen
relationship between wealthy cast members and their servants. This class relationship is mapped onto spatial coordinates onscreen and helps to define the
rich bitch as normative, although still insufferable at points. The spatialization
of the elite and their servants allows us to laugh at the rich and still see their
world as normative and desirable. Interaction with servants defines the rich
people on Bravo as responsible property owners, astute entrepreneurs, good
romantic partners, sound psychological counselors, and whole people.

THE DEGENERATE SERVER: *VANDERPUMP RULES*, ORIENTALISM, AND THE NORMALIZATION OF THE RICH THROUGH GEOGRAPHY

No other reality show displays the geographies of the rich and their servers with such extensive detail as *Vanderpump Rules*. For every scene in Lisa

Vanderpump's luxurious mansion, the program shows another scene in an unspectacular apartment of one of her servers. The program does not map out these parts of contemporary cites separately. Rather, it constructs a relationship between these two areas, one similar to the geographic association between the West and the East theorized by post-colonial scholar Edward Said in *Orientalism*. Said's monumental study of western domination over the East maintains that geographies are human made, not natural. The creation of two areas linked through uneven power relations allows one to dominate, restructure, and exert authority over the other. This occurs because subordinate groups are othered in order to make them knowable and controllable. A social group outside of the realm of the dominant is placed in a partnership where it is the weak to the dominant's strong. Thus, the othered groups do not exist as themselves. They become a fantasy version of themselves for the dominant group. As others, they are in need of correction through institutions such as law, education, and government.[8] This is what is known as *hegemony*: the way various institutions form a loose network of power both to control a dominated social group and to win its consent. Said's use of hegemony incorporates Michael Foucault's concepts of normality and abnormality. Foucault argues there is nothing natural about what society deems as normal. Rather, the normal is constructed by an articulation of legal, medical, scientific, religious, and educational institutions that define certain groups and identities as normal and others as abnormal.[9] What makes Lisa Vanderpump a redemptive figure of wealth on *Vanderpump Rules* is that these various institutions of social control become centralized around her. She functions as the psychiatrist, educator, medical doctor, and law enforcer who controls her othered service staff. Her restaurant and home, two locales of Los Angeles' political economy of social expulsions, become centralized places of normality from which she can diagnose her servers as abnormal.

Sur and Lisa's home function as spaces of normalization on the show, in part because Lisa's confessionals are shot in both locations and play a crucial role discursively constructing her servers as backward. For example, Lisa often refers to her servers (who are in their late twenties and early thirties) as bad children who need her mothering. In the "This Is a Break-Up" episode, Lisa sits in Sur, reflecting on bickering between servers on a Sur float at a gay pride parade. She bemoans that she had to raise her own children and now she has to raise her employees. In the "I'm Not a Bitch" episode, Lisa calls a staff meeting at Sur after her servers get into a brawl at a Las Vegas bar. She tells them they act like high school children and need to grow up. Lisa also others her employees by saying there is no in-company dating at Sur. The hilarity of this comment is that nearly every server on the show is dating someone at Sur. Season One opens with Stassi dating Jax and Kristen dating Tom Sandoval. Lisa's confessionals do more than point out how her servers violate company dating policy. She portrays them as perverse and often jokingly speculates that her employees have orgies with each other.

Figure 3.1 Lisa Vanderpump poses on mansion grounds.
Bravo/Photofest ©Bravo

Vanderpump Rules also normalizes the space of Sur by showing how the servers fit beautifully into the luxury economy there but live in rundown apartments that demystify their glamour and reveal their true class status. At Sur, the bartenders wear sharp, long-sleeve black button ups, and the waitresses wear slim-cut, trendy black dresses. They stand out against the white modern decor of Sur and are, in fact, part of the color scheme of the establishment. The bartenders work at counters decorated with expensive floral arrangements, and the waitresses bring expensive, beautifully decorated meals to wealthy, stylish clients. The interior of Sur is at once extravagant yet modern. In Season One, the apartments the servers live in are drab. Kristen and Tom's apartment has stained white carpet and dirty white walls. The kitchen cabinets, low-end white with natural wood trim, were popular in many budget apartments during the 1990s. The appliances are noticeably old and worn. Many scenes in apartments include dialogue that highlights how unworldly and unsophisticated the servers are. When Kristen and Stassi decide to apply for passports in Season One, Kristen says she's never had a passport photo taken, but she has had her mugshot taken. Season Four opens with Jax's mother coming from Los Angeles to visit him. He explains how most things in his apartment were stolen from Sur.

Many scenes at Lisa's house also have servers jointly fitting into the world of luxury and also being excluded from it, both for their economic and cultural power. The episode "Last Call" follows Lisa creating a publicity campaign for Sur's summer business. She brings in her servers for a poolside shot. The servers dress in designer clothes and skimpy bathing suits for which Lisa paid, and the women servers also wear Lisa's jewelry. While they embody the expensive and sexual image of Sur, Kristen Doute says in a confessional that none of the servers could ever afford the clothes they are modeling since they are all broke. Likewise, in a scene from Season Four, Tom Sandoval and Tom Schwartz are at Lisa's house to discuss their (doomed for failure) attempts to help build the Pump Sangria brand when they, alone in a room, see a framed artistic nude picture of Lisa and say they plan to masturbate to that image later that night—demonstrating that they cannot comprehend a nude as a form of highbrow art, only as a form of lowbrow pornography.

Within Sur, Lisa keeps the behavior of her servers in check by functioning as a psychologist, police office, medical doctor, and career counselor in an effort to correct the abnormal behavior of her employees. For example, in Season Two, many episodes include her meeting with Jax like a counselor and talking to him about his pathological lying and serial cheating. She advises him to confront his issues head on or he will never improve as a person and have healthy relationships. In fact, Jax graduates from his discussions with Lisa by going to see a psychologist. In Season Four, Lisa functions as a medical doctor who understands drug and alcohol addiction when she consoles her server Scheana about her husband's addiction to prescription pain pills. She calls Scheana naïve when the server says she wants her husband to stop taking pain pills but to continue drinking when they go out. Lisa tells Scheana she has no idea about the complexities of addiction—that addicts cannot socialize around addictive substances. She tells Scheana that she has to see her husband as an addict and not as an accessory to her desired social life. Lisa's advice is often biting, condescending, and full of class-based disgust. For example, when Stassi is missing writing deadlines for the fashion blog that Lisa's daughter runs, Stassi claims that writing is her hobby and not a job. Lisa retorts that hobbies are for rich people who have jobs. What Stassi needs is a job. This is an interesting statement, for it not only suggests that those beneath Lisa deserve no pleasure in their time off but that Stassi's own work at Sur is, in fact, not a form of valid labor. Lisa takes on the role of police when Jax gets arrested for shoplifting a pair of designer sunglasses while on vacation in Hawaii in Season Four. When Jax flies back to Los Angeles, he must have a special meeting with Lisa at her house, at which point she disciplines him by putting him on indefinite suspension and telling him that his behavior risks him being banned from Sur.

Spaces outside of Sur and Lisa's home become places where servers are at risk of becoming uncivilized. The "Vegas With a Vengeance" episode spatializes proper and improper romances by contrasting the appropriately expressed love of Lisa's daughter, Pandora, at Lisa's house versus the inappropriately expressed love of Jax at a Las Vegas casino. The scene at Lisa's house opens in Ken's office, which is detached from the house and has pictures of yachts on the walls and floor-to-ceiling windows overlooking a garden. Lisa comes in and tells Ken she just received Pandora's wedding video in the mail and would like to watch it with him. The couple then walks across their well-manicured lawn. Their pack of Pomeranians dressed in designer dog clothes follows them. The two then retreat to their home movie theatre and watch the wedding on the big screen. Johann Pachelbel's classical piece "Canon in D" plays as Pandora looks in the mirror at Lisa's estate and then heads down the mansion's spiral stair case. The video cuts to her husband Jason standing at the altar, looking properly aristocratic. The scene then cuts to Lisa in their movie theatre as she says, "There is the father to my future grandchildren." The scene is strategically placed between two in which the servers demonstrate lewdness and a complete lack of civility in Las Vegas. In the prior scene, Jax surprises his ex-girlfriend Stassi as he comes to her birthday party at a Las Vegas bar, where Stassi is with her friends from Sur and her new boyfriend, Tom, also a bartender at Sur. Within a few minutes, a brawl breaks out when Stassi throws a drink in Tom Schwartz's face for standing up for Jax, and bartender Tom and Jax have to be separated to stop a fist fight. The conversation quickly becomes vulgar, as Jax tells bartender Tom "enjoy the taste of my dick" and "you're a pussy." As the fight spills into the club's parking lot, Jax, Tom Sandoval, and Stassi's boyfriend Tom take their shirts off and begin to charge each other, as the production crew and onlookers try to separate the men. Their semi-naked bodies in a public space contrast with the sharply dressed classiness of Lisa's husband as they watch the wedding video. The scene following Pandora's wedding video has Stassi, Kristen, Katie, and bartender Tom climb over the fence of a closed hotel pool and proceed to skinny dip and lewdly talk about who is touching whose genitalia.

The show also visualizes spaces at Sur available only to servers, not to customers, in an effort to show how classed behaviors at Sur are to be kept at bay. Nearly every episode contains scenes where servers take breaks and smoke cigarettes in the alley behind Sur. Season Four, for example, has many scenes where busboy and Sur DJ James Kennedy takes breaks to talk to his girlfriend Kristen Doute, who has been fired from Sur by then. Typical scenes include James calling Kristen misogynistic terms such as slut and bitch while Kristen calls him pathetic and jealous. The mise-en-scene adds to the different classed space here, as all we see are dumpsters from Sur and other restaurants. This marks their outlandish behavior as part of the hidden economy of luxury, an economy that needs trash pick-up and servitude but does not want to place it in plain sight to ruin the glamourous look of West Hollywood.

The show suggests that Lisa's status as employer gives her the right to control her servers' behavior outside of her restaurant and her home. For example, in the episode after the Las Vegas fight, Lisa calls a staff meeting and tells them, "When you are all there, as a body, as a group, you are actually representing my restaurant. Sur was there [in Las Vegas]. And that is what really upsets me." This puts the servers in a double bind. On the one hand, their behavior in the previous episode legitimizes Lisa and Ken's vision of romance as appropriate. On the other, this episode suggests that Lisa's control of the servers extends beyond the confines of her branded businesses, because the servers are themselves part of the branded business.

Vanderpump Rules' extended investigation into servers' lives is reliant upon the blurred lines that the people who work at Sur are and are not servers. Even though the program represents the servers as in need of correction, it also defines them as worthy of watching because they aspire to be more than servers. The episode "Caught with Your Trousers Down" begins with a five-minute montage narrated with a confession by Kristen Doute where she explains how every server is actively trying to make it in music, film, theatre, or modeling. As the montage goes from Scheana singing to Kristen rehearsing a scene to Tina working at a photo shoot to Tom Sandoval playing guitar at a club to Jax looking at a sunglasses ad featuring him to Peter screening a film he produced, Kristen says, "Lisa told me that working at Sur is not what she wants for any of us for the rest of our lives." This partly sets up Lisa's brand as so extravagant it excludes the true serving class of global cities. Her brand is to have the future elite of Los Angeles serve the current elite.

Despite this, there are discursive struggles within the series to define cast members merely as servers to show their personal and professional failures, a strategy easy to enact because none of the main cast members have broken into the entertainment industry enough to leave Sur. In the "Instafight" episode, Lisa complains to her manager Peter that all of the shifts aren't covered; Peter claims that is because many servers have auditions. Lisa responds that her employees "need a strong kick in the ass" to get them focussed on their jobs at Sur. The "Tooth or Consequences" episode includes an amusingly hypocritical statement from Lisa after Kristen misbehaves at a catered event. Lisa says, "These girls need to understand that they are just here to serve.

They don't need to provide the entertainment." Since the show is about the melodrama among the servers at Sur, of course they are there to provide entertainment. But Lisa's statement shows how the idea of the server can be used to assert her control. This same discourse is used as a means of distinction among the servers. Season One ends with a marginal character, Laura Leigh, quitting Sur because she landed a role in the Jennifer Aniston film *We're the Millers*. In her departing confessional, she notes that, while she is leaving serving behind, her troubled boyfriend and Sur bartender Jax will spend the rest of his life as a server. In the "Branded" episode, Stassi says in a confessional that she evolves but that Tom Sandoval and Kristen Doute do not. Years from now they will still be servers living in their same crummy apartment. To be a server is to be an object of disgust.

The way the servers exist at the intersections of being a server and not being a server mirrors the way they exist at the intersection of race, nationality, and class on the show. Although servers are part of Bravo's other programs, *Vanderpump Rules* is the only show on the channel with white servers. Other servers are typically Mexican or Hispanic. Thus, the servers on *Vanderpump Rules* are an example of what Richard Dyer says about whiteness: that it is both invisible through its universality and it is a visible passport to privilege.[10] Although Bravo never mentions race in its psychographic claims in the trades and although race is never explicitly mentioned in shows, Bravo presents a world of wealthy white people who have non-white servants. That the servers on *Vanderpump Rules* have the opportunity to speak is because they have white privilege to consider careers beyond serving. George Lipsitz argues that, although race is a delusion that has no grounding in biology or anthropology, "White Americans are encouraged to invest in whiteness, to remain true to an identity that provides them with resources, power, and opportunity."[11] Lipsitz examines how whiteness carries with it advantages in society in terms of housing markets, educational opportunities, employment options, and networking. Whiteness gives the servers at Sur opportunities that servers on other Bravo shows don't have. But Lisa's British upper-class, refined demeanor actually delegitimizes the feasibility of her servers' success by showing them as lowbrow Americans who are so consumed with bodily pleasures—overindulging in alcohol, getting naked, having too much sex— that they can't intellectually grasp how to be successful entrepreneurs.

These contradictions simultaneously call for Lisa to control her backward servers and authenticate Sur's brand as a place to bring your mistress. As she states in Episode One, "Villa Blanca [Lisa's other restaurant] is a place to take your wife. Sur is a place to take your mistress." *Vanderpump Rules* shows that while Sur looks pretty and romantic on the inside, it is full of juicy gossip and scandal that remain unseen to those in the restaurant. Any server who happily takes your order has probably just come from a fight with a jolted lover, a romantic tryst with a coworker, or a scandalous weekend in Las Vegas where cheating took place. These servers are perfect for Sur's brand of illicit relationships and naughty sexuality.

Sur becomes a space that demonstrates Lisa's successful entrepreneurship and her servers' failed entrepreneurial adventures. *Vanderpump Rules* serves as a vehicle for Lisa to establish her brand. Lisa's brand is elegance, whether that is catering to typical domesticity or a spicy love life. *Vanderpump Rules* follows Lisa as she extends her brand as well. In Season Two she buys the adjoining store property next to Sur and remodels it to open a new bar area in her restaurant. Season Three follows her successful opening of Pump, a gay bar and restaurant in West Hollywood. Season Four follows Lisa, her daughter, and her son-in-law as they take Lisa's own sangria from a drink served at her restaurants to an international product. Additionally, *Vanderpump Rules* shows Lisa as a working woman. Episodes include her shopping for floral arrangements for Sur, and scenes often begin with servers approaching Lisa while she is redecorating her business before it opens. *Vanderpump Rules* gives insight into how Lisa affords her luxurious lifestyle on *The Real Housewives of Beverly Hills*.

Lisa's servers at Sur try to follow their employer's path to successful entrepreneurship, but they are abject failures at it. In Season Four, bartender Tom Sandoval and Tom Schwartz, unemployed boyfriend of Sur waitress Katie Maloney, propose to Lisa that they will become brand ambassadors for her new sangria. In a comical scene, the Toms set up an appointment with Lisa, her daughter, and her son-in-law to let them know they often party in Sandoval's home city of St. Louis and would love to take several bottles with them to share when they go out to bars there. Lisa then explains that her daughter has had meetings with distributors in Europe and Australia and has developed a business plan to make Pump Sangria an international product.

After Lisa chides the Toms for not taking business seriously, she asks them how they could help in this international distribution plan, and the Toms come across as bigger idiots when they maintain that their partying in St. Louis with Pump Sangria will help just as much as Pandora's business plans. The season delightfully follows Lisa as she tries to take on the Toms and mentor them as entrepreneurs, only to have both quit because neither has the drive to succeed.

Another failed entrepreneurship happens when Scheana tries to launch a singing career. Stassi calls Scheana a drunk, slutty, pathetic Brittany Spears rip off. Episodes that focus on Scheana's singing typically include studio sessions where producers get the aspiring artist to moan into the microphone in a way that makes it sound like she is recording pornography vocals. Other episodes show Stassi as a failure at fashion blogging, opting to get drunk and lounge at a pool instead of meeting her writing deadlines. Even servers who have moderate success branding themselves as entertainers outside of the show are depicted as being pathetic. For example, Katie's boyfriend Tom Schwartz starts Season One as a model with some consistent employment, but by Season Four his body shows the effects of heavy drinking. Photographers have to photoshop his beer belly out of pictures. Likewise, bartender Ariana and server Kristen try to brand themselves as sketch comedy artists, but rather than show their actual sketch work, *Vanderpump Rules* includes scenes where the two women gossip behind the other's back about how untalented the other is. Unlike Lisa, who stays focussed on her vision, Ariana and Kristen get diverted through jealousy and misguided energy.

Ultimately, the failures of the servers to develop a brand mark Lisa's world as the norm: a world where everyone strives for professional excellence. Yet the only person who has truly achieved it, who can actualize the values presented on the show, is Lisa. Her successes as a businesswoman, psychologist, medical doctor, and police person are cemented through the way that she helps, guides, teaches, or contrasts with her servers, all of whom are failures and need help. The geographies of affluence and servitude exist in a relationship where the former gains normative powers through the deviance found in the latter.

THE SILENT SERVANT: THE NOBLE SAVAGE IN THE CITY ON *THE REAL HOUSEWIVES*

Although the servers on *Vanderpump Rules* are so loud and obnoxious that they appear to be descendants of contestants on *The Jerry Springer Show* (1991–present), *The Real Housewives* franchise also presents us with the silent servant: the hired help who typically works in the home of elite cast members and almost goes unnoticed. Over the course of a season these servants might have lines in a scene or two, but mostly they exist in the background of shows. Two things set them apart from the servers on *Vanderpump Rules*: they are portrayed as good people who know their roles, and they are not white. This is a different form of othering on Bravo programming, as it changes the servant from an immoral person in need of correction to a moral person who exists only to serve the elite. Here Bravo others servants through the trope of the noble savage, a figure that Ter Ellingson claims originated in the eighteenth century to show how native, non-white people were innately good because they have been uncorrupted by civilizing forces.[12] Bravo's rendition of the noble savage differs from eighteenth-century tales in that the figure is not found on native grounds but within global cities. Accordingly, the noble savage exists in a power relationship with the elite, either by existing as a "natural" part of the extravagant mise-en-scene of wealth or by taking on domestic chores so that his or her elite employers can move through the city for leisure and enjoyment. Thus, non-white servants become positioned in space as natives on the grounds of their employers, and the desires they express are the desires of the rich, not their own.

The introduction to Adrienne Maloof's servant Bernie in the "It's My Party and I'll Spend if I Want to" episode of *The Real Housewives of Beverly Hills* shows the dual function of the noble savage in the franchise. First, Bernie exists as part of the natural beauty on Adrienne's exquisitely manicured property. Nature discursively exists on the show not through forests or unaltered landscapes but through expensive landscaping that highlights the wealth of the elite. The scene integrates civilization, wealth, and nature at Adrienne's property, and Bernie becomes associated with nature that demonstrates Adrienne's wealth. The first two shots of the scene present civilization in the foreground of the screen and natural beauty in the background. The scene opens with an exterior shot of Adrienne's front yard. In the foreground is a wraparound driveway, and in the center is a three-tiered fountain supported by four exquisitely sculpted lions. Immediately what stands out is that the driveway is built by a talented architect. This is a space of coming and going for the Beverly Hills elite. Even so, the fountain attempts to blend the harmony of nature's flowing water into a designed space. The background of the frame dwarfs the fountain, as Adrienne's two-story stucco Beverly Hills mansion ends the horizon. Nature adorns civilization again. There are six additional fountains bordering the front of the house along with shrubs and flowering bushes bordering the driveway. The next shot again uses the foreground-background structure, only here civilization is squarely in the foreground and nature fills in the background. Paul, Adrienne's husband, puts helmets on their two children on a porch in the front right of the frame. Columns in the back of the house go from Paul in the front corner all the way to the back of the right frame, drawing the viewer's attention to the back of the screen. There open fields of beautiful grass bordered by trees and bushes dominate our sight. Shot three, which captures Adrienne entering her backyard, shifts the emphasis between nature and civilization in the background and foreground. Adrienne enters from the rear right of the screen as she proceeds to walk past the chef and toward her husband. The dining area is just as beautiful as Adrienne's fountains in the front yard, and Chef Bernie signifies nature through the othering, racist representational strategy that non-whites represent the uncivilized. He blends with the architectural beauty of the well-designed outdoor kitchen.

As the scene progresses, Bernie takes on a nobility through the way his calm and gentle demeanor contrasts with the tumultuous relationships in the Maloof family. The editing cuts from Bernie calmly preparing lunch for the Maloofs to confessionals of Adrienne talking about how rocky it is to be a mom, to shots of the children fighting, and to Paul walking away from lunch out of anger. Moreover, what produces anger in the scene directly relates to civilization. Adrienne notes that Paul has a short temper with the children after he gets home from work, and she finds it trying to manage a career and family. Bernie's work places him at peace because, in the show, he exists as part of the natural beauty of the property, not as a worker in Los Angeles' global economy.

The second half of the scene shows how Bernie's noble savagery becomes a tool of benevolence to extend Adrienne's personhood. The scene presents very conventional notions of gender and domestic labor. Even though Adrienne's husband Paul Nasif is a famous Beverly Hills plastic surgeon, both he and Adrienne mention openly that she makes significantly more money than him. Still, Adrienne says in a confessional in this scene that she is a woman who takes care of the house and presents her husband as a professional who can't be bothered with domestic duties. But Adrienne says she needs help to be a good mom, as she relies on a chef, nanny, and maid. At that point, we cut to footage of Adrienne standing behind the outdoor bar and serving plates of food that Bernie prepared to her children and husband. There are two layers to Bernie's nobility here. First, his sincerity in food preparation foils Adrienne's hypocrisy, as Bernie actually performs his job as a chef, whereas Adrienne pawns off her responsibilities that she attempts to own as a mother. Second, Bernie's benevolence exists solely to help Adrienne accomplish her goals. He never receives any screen time to express his own identity. He merely helps Adrienne construct her own identity as a domestic mother.

Servants don't have to serve the dual function that Bernie does for Adrienne; sometimes they are in *The Real Housewives* just to be part of the uncorrupted natural beauty in a world of hypocritical rich opulence. For example, the same episode of the Beverly Hills season also features Taylor Armstrong throwing a $60,000 birthday party for her four-year-old daughter. The episode uses editing to show how Taylor's daughter cares nothing about the party and that the event is merely an opportunity for Taylor to demonstrate her wealth to her adult friends. The party itself, though, is slightly more ambiguous because the shot sequence admittedly displays the natural beauty of the party while still highlighting Taylor's hypocrisy. Taylor rents the luxurious Houdini Estate in the Laurel Canons, and the scene opens with a montage of the mansion, the fountains, and the grounds. The mansion sits on the highest point on the property, and a steep hill landscaped with palm trees, flowers, and bushes is adorned with several balconies and a few opulent stair cases. At the bottom of the hill is a flat area with perfectly green grass. There sits a table with a pink tent. The table integrates the party into nature through the way it is adorned with pink roses, rose petals laying on teacup coasters, and tiny bushes sculpted to look like tea pots. At the end of the montage is a shot of three Hispanic servants peacefully smiling with their arms all held straight down and tight against their bodies. They demonstrate the tranquility of the property. The scene then edits in footage of Taylor talking to her friend and party planner Dwight about how wonderful the party is while Taylor's daughter hides in the house and is unenthused about the event. In a confessional, Dwight says that Taylor is a great, hands-on mother, and then the scene edits in Taylor's daughter coming down to the party, asking to leave, and Taylor forcing her to take a picture. The conflict within Taylor—her anger toward her daughter for not caring, her enthusiasm with her white friends for the party—contrasts with the peacefulness of the noble servants.

The Real Housewives of New York City uses the trope of the noble savage for the Countess Luann de Lesseps' live-in nanny/maid Rosie in order to make her merely an extension of Luann's personhood. In Season Two, while Luann is still married to the Count and splitting her time between their Upper East Side townhome and their Hamptons mansion, it is common for Luann to give Rosie instructions on how to parent her son and daughter before she goes out on the town. While Luann goes out for nights full of melodramatic fighting with her rich friends, Rosie peacefully parents Luann's children. The "Hamptons Retreat . . . But No Surrender" episode shows various ways that the noble savage is at peace in the natural existence of the home. Rosie returns from a trip home to visit her family in the Philippines. The program positions the Philippines as a place of tranquility. When Luann and her children ask Rosie how her visit home was, she responds in generalities such as "great." But when Rosie asks how things went without her, Luann depicts her home as a place of conflict, noting she was stressed out and lost weight because she had to do the domestic chores that Rosie does. After that, Luann takes Rosie downstairs and shows her all the laundry she needs to do right away. Luann then states, "All right, Rosie. You get organized, and I am going to play tennis." Now that her servant is home, Luanne's personal responsibilities shift so Luann can socialize. Rosie's ability to perform domestic labor fits into the natural order of things and frees Luann to go experience deserved leisure in civilized society.

Sexuality and feelings also figure into the nobility of the non-white, silent servants, for their only ability to express emotions and desires is through sympathy toward their employers. For example, in Season Three of the New York series, Rosie, who lives in an outer borough, can no longer work for Luann after Luann gets divorced and moves full time to her Hamptons house. But when Rosie comes for a visit in the Hamptons, Rosie expresses emotion, but only of her understanding of Luann's emotional state after a divorce. She states, "Mrs. D seems like she's tough, you know from the outside, but of course, deep inside, you know, she's lonely." Rosie's naturalness allows her to see past the façade of Luann's seemingly happy life in a Hamptons estate and understand her true feelings. But silent servants are never allowed to vocalize their own pain or their own emotions about the state of their lives and perhaps the hardships that they go through. Moreover, part of what makes them noble is that they are the exact opposite of the amorous servers at Sur on *Vanderpump Rules*. They never have any sexual desires and are castrated or desexualized figures.

Geography naturalizes the world view that cities should be made up of elites and their silent servants through the contradictory equation of the noble savage with the natural beauty of urban estates. This is built upon an illogical foundation, for the areas of "natural beauty" where the silent servants work are, in fact, human made and meticulously landscaped by paid servants. Thus, the naturalness of the noble savages—the connection with uncivilized nature—is false, for they are one with manicured spaces built through the money of the very corrupt elite who employ the servants. If silent servants bear any resemblance to nature on the show, it is that they are shaped to please the rich, just like the landscaping of the estate is professionally shaped.

THE SILLY SERVANT: HISPANIC AND LATINA STEREOTYPES AS GEOGRAPHIC CONTAINMENT/EXPULSION

Servants shoehorned into the stereotype of noble savage range in non-white racial categories from Asian to Latina, but many Latina and Hispanic characters fall more squarely within stereotypes of their own race when portrayed as domestic servants on Bravo reality programming. This is especially the case when the servant is portrayed as silly and used for moments of comic relief in programs. Depending on the stereotype used, though, the servant is either positioned as belonging squarely within the homes of the elite or depicted as morally corrupt and in need of expulsion from white spaces.

Cedric Martinez in Season One of *The Real Housewives of Beverly Hills* exists at the crossroads of several stereotypes used for Hispanic characters. Martinez is Lisa's servant who lives on the Vanderpump estate in Lisa's guest house. Martinez claims to have been born in France to a prostitute who got pregnant while working. Although his exact ethnic and racial background is impossible to tell, given his partly unknown parentage, it is clear that Cedric is part of a larger immigration movement whereby Spaniards spread throughout Europe. Cedric is included in the scene of Episode One of Season One that introduces Lisa to the audience, and immediately he takes on the stereotype of the Latin lover. Charles Ramirez Berg identifies this as a character "who is the possessor of a primal sexuality that ma[kes] him capable of making a sensuous but dangerous—and clearly non-WASP—brand of love."[13] The scene introduces Lisa as someone who values her house—she states she has so much there is no reason to ever leave—but also devalues sex with her husband, restaurateur Ken Todd. Lisa states, "Ken calls me a sex object. He says every time he wants sex, I object. I say to him, it's Christmas and birthdays. And I say to him, it's your birthday, not mine, that's another day off." While Ken explains the dynamics of their relationship in confessionals, the scene edits in footage of them talking to each other in their house. They are on different floors of their mansion, calling to each other, as the sound echoes through their cavernous home. Their sexuality is portrayed as WASP-y and very reserved, made even more visible by their refined rich clothes that downplay their bodies. However, Cedric's introduction is incredibly sexual. The scene cuts to Lisa and Cedric in workout clothes in a way that flaunts their bodies. As Lisa and Cedric work out in her home gym and evaluate the beauty of each other's body, Lisa talks in a confessional about how Cedric was the face of one of their gay clubs in London and then moved to Los Angeles with them. Ken then comments in a confessional that he hopes Cedric is gay, otherwise he is probably having an affair with Lisa. Although there is a tongue-in-cheek element of Ken's remark, the workout footage gives it more weight through the way Cedric shares a sensual chemistry with Lisa that Ken does not.

The scene activates another stereotype, the male buffoon, through the way that Cedric is positioned as a substitute for Lisa and Ken's children, who have grown up and left home. Ramirez Berg claims this figure stands apart from WASP-y culture for being both simple-minded and regressing into emotional childlike states.[14] Cedric's puerile vanity shows through his obsession with his own body and his insecurity when he asks Lisa if certain muscles look good. Cedric's childlike immaturity also appears in the episode "My Mansion Is Bigger Than Your Mansion" when Lisa and her British-Middle-Eastern friend Mohammed throw a dinner party. The episode balances WASP culture against the non-white other. While Mohammed's mansion is typical of Beverly Hills, his basement has a Middle-Eastern decor. After the party ends outside, the party retires to Mohammed's basement, where, by chance, Cedric is naked in a hot tub. Rather than show restraint, a quality that structures the dinner party, he walks out of the hot tub naked for the entire party to see, which helps transition the evening toward Middle-Eastern dancing with hired belly dancers.

Ken's fears that Cedric might be stealing Lisa from him activate another stereotype: the bandito or the bandit. Angharad N. Valdivia argues the bandito "forms the basis for more recent representation of Latinos as criminals."[15] Cedric comes across as a thief on numerous levels, from his potential to steal Lisa from Ken by pretending to be gay to his conning Lisa by performing the role of victim of circumstance—the poor, lost man abandoned by his prostitute mother, in order to live in a Beverly Hills mansion. But in the finale of Season One, Ken erects barriers between servant and residence when he says, "He treats this home like his own home, and I'm sick of it. I wouldn't take this type of behavior from my children, and I won't take it from a thirty-seven-year-old man." For Ken, servants do not belong in the home. Cedric is stealing Lisa from Ken, he is stealing money from Ken through unpaid rent, and he is robbing Ken of a proper marriage, since his presence there changes the way Ken interacts with his wife.

If, as Ramirez Berg argues, the bandito displays vulgarity as he viciously pursues money and power, this racializing of betrayal marks proper and improper pandering to the tabloids on *The Real Housewives of Beverly Hills*.

Cedric's behavior is marked as vicious when he explodes at Lisa while he is moving out by the end of the finale. Ken's request to have his marriage back leads to such violent behavior that Lisa and Cedric never speak again. Moreover, Cedric sells stories to the tabloids about cast members in a way that is coded as only mean spirited. He claims Adrienne Maloof was going bankrupt and that Kim Richards' addiction to drugs and alcohol was worse than it appeared to be on the show. Season Two opens with Cedric being portrayed as a rat for his tabloid stories, but interestingly, Lisa is frequently accused of selling stories to the tabloids in Seasons One and Two because her best friend is the editor at US Weekly. When Lisa is accused of these doings, cast members claim that Lisa is a good business woman who knows how to make money from stories from the show, or Lisa claims that the stories she sold were ultimately meant to help women overcome serious problems, such as Taylor Armstrong's suffering from domestic violence and Camille Grammer going through a divorce. In fact, Taylor becomes best friends with Lisa in Season Two because Armstrong comes to believe that Lisa genuinely cares about her. Cedric's theft, then, shows that the leaking of stories is coded as right or wrong depending on race and class status.

When Cedric is kicked out of Ken and Lisa's home at the end of Season One, he becomes a racialized scapegoat for many of the behaviors that the real housewives actually exhibit themselves. Many of the women are gold diggers who live off their husband's money. They backstab each other and leak stories, but they are allowed to do this. Cedric's racialization make those same traits worthy of expulsion.

While The Real Housewives of Beverly Hills uses stereotypes of Hispanic people to remove the servant from the land of the rich, Flipping Out uses the stereotype of the Latina maid to confine the servant to domestic spaces and limit her access to the city. Valdivia argues the maid is a relatively new image for Latinas in the media and doesn't have the historical weight that the figures of the harlot, the female clown, or the dark lady do. The Latina domestic borrows traits from the African American mammy figure prominent in twentieth-century imagery, in that she can be either buffoonish and young or caring and willing to sacrifice her own life to care for others.[16] Valdivia argues the Latina maid often exists so that upper-middle-class white people can enjoy leisure. Flipping Out borrows on this imagery of the buffoonish

Latina maid, but it uniquely inflects the maid's relationship to whiteness since Jeff works from home and has his employees work in his house. Thus, Jeff's maid Zoila's domestic work occurs within the same space as Jeff's other employees. Zoila differs, though, from Jeff's other employees in that she does not leave the house, while the others go with Jeff to remodel houses. Zoila's domestic confinement in many ways makes her more able to deal with Jeff's demeaning OCD tendencies that make the tiniest details gain monumental and stressful significance. As the Latina maid, she is equipped with stereotypical characteristics that allow her to laugh at Jeff's stressful quirks, while many other cast members express frustration that these traits, in fact, stunt their abilities to grow as professionals. As a result, Jeff's characteristics become both a source of benevolence and frustration to white cast members but also a source of humor to Zoila.

The "Urine Trouble" episode demonstrates this dynamic. The episode focuses on Jeff's behavior leading to a potential fallout with clients and his employees. The first scene has Jeff going to meet with Christie, the owner of the Casa Vega restaurant that Jeff is remodeling. After Christie confesses that she feels overwhelmed and under supported in her renovation, as she struggles to deal with the demands of mothering and co-owning a business with her father, Jeff says in a confessional he needs to be a better person and be there more for his clients because remodeling is stressful. In a later scene Jeff belittles his part-time assistant Trace when he accuses him of doing homework at work. Like restaurateur Christie, Trace is genuinely hurt by Jeff's biting words, and the rest of the episode includes footage of Jeff making it up to Trace by taking him on his very best jobs, such as a private jet trip to Northern California for a client, and telling Trace he will now groom him as a fulltime employee. Zoila receives none of the niceties that Jeff's clients and assistants get, but her Latina maid stereotype make her suited to absorb Jeff's difficulties in the home. In this episode, she helps Jeff repel coyotes coming onto his property by dousing the property lines with urine, a strategy that Jeff read online will make the animals think this territory belongs to another animal and is off limits. But the joke of the episode is that, while Jeff could buy coyote pee online, he chooses to save the money by having his employees pee in bottles that Zoila will help him pour along the property lines. When Jeff hands a seemingly empty bottle of urine back

Figure 3.2 Jeff and Zoila on *Flipping Out*.
Bravo/Photofest ©Bravo

to Zoila, the container leaks extra urine onto Zoila's hands and clothes. Zoila laughs and says "God dammit, Jeffrey." Then Jeff says, "We have a serious coyote problem, and that is what I'm trying to solve right now. I'm trying to keep the coyotes away from you. I did you a favor." Zoila absorbs his neurosis by saying, in broken English, "You funny, Jeffrey." Jeff offers Zoila no professional advancement within the episode because, as a Latina servant, she is immune to Jeff's neurotic behavior. In other episodes where Jeff does something nice for Zoila, it is by throwing her a party—not offering her new employment opportunities. Thus, Zoila's job naturalizes her limited access to the city. She is part of a political economy of expulsions, but her duties and abilities to deal with Jeff keep her confined to the home, whereas other employees progress to travel the city for professional advancement.

CONCLUSION

It's rare for servants and servers to appear on contemporary reality programs about city life, despite the fact that servants and servers make up a crucial demographic of cities during the era of social expulsions. Bravo's continual efforts to televise the lives of urban servants and servers warrants an extended analysis in order to understand why a channel about the rich would invest so much time in tales about their servants and servers. As Bravo handles two contradictory branding initiatives—lauding the rich and mocking them—their shows stabilize a positive presentation of the geographies of affluence through a denigration of the geographies of servitude. The degenerate server, the silent servant, and the silly servant activate different geographic relationships between the rich and their servants/servers in order to normalize the rich through the othering of the poor. These geographic negotiations help to win our consent for the political economy of social expulsions, as they frame the urban elite as the norm for us. Bravo is not unique, however, in presenting economically vulnerable groups on reality television. The next chapter looks at how two stars—Rob Mariano and Tiffany Pollard—built reality personas by performing identities of economically vulnerable ethnic and racial groups, and how such performances became ways to chart successful reality gaming careers.

NOTES

1 Joseph Turow, *Breaking Up America: Advertisers and the New Media World* (Chicago, IL: University of Chicago Press, 1997), 102–10.
2 Catherine Johnson, *Branding Television* (New York: Routledge, 2012), 167.
3 Amanda Ann Klein, "MTV Reality Programming and the Labor of Identity," *CST Online*, May 23, 2013. Accessed August 8, 2016. http://cstonline.tv/mtv;

Erin Copple Smith, "'Affluencers' by Bravo: Defining an Audience Through Cross Promotion," *Popular Communication* 10 (2012), 286–301.

4 Erin Copple Smith, "'Affluencers' by Bravo: Defining an Audience Through Cross Promotion," *Popular Communication* 10 (2012), 292.

5 Erin Copple Smith, "'Affluencers' by Bravo: Defining an Audience Through Cross Promotion," *Popular Communication* 10 (2012), 292.

6 Quoted in Michael J. Lee and Leigh Moscowitz, "The 'Rich Bitch': Class and Gender on *The Real Housewives of New York City*," *Feminist Media Studies* 13, no. 1 (2013), 68.

7 Quoted in Michael J. Lee and Leigh Moscowitz, "The 'Rich Bitch': Class and Gender on *The Real Housewives of New York City*," *Feminist Media Studies* 13, no. 1 (2013), 64–82.

8 Edward Said, *Orientalism* (New York: Pantheon, 1978).

9 Michel Foucault, *Discipline and Punish: The Birth of the Prison*, trans. Alan Sheridan (New York: Vintage, 1979).

10 Richard Dyer, *White: Essays on Race and Culture* (New York: Routledge, 1997), 46–50.

11 George Lipsitz, *The Possessive Investment in Whiteness: How White People Profit from Identity Politics*, Revised and Expanded Edition (Philadelphia, PA: Temple University Press, 2006), vii.

12 Ter Ellingson, *The Myth of the Noble Savage* (Berkeley, CA: University of California Press, 2001).

13 Charles Ramirez Berg, *Latino Images in Film: Stereotypes, Subversion, and Resistance* (Austin: University of Texas Press, 2002), 76.

14 Charles Ramirez Berg, *Latino Images in Film: Stereotypes, Subversion, and Resistance* (Austin, TX: University of Texas Press, 2002), 71–3.

15 Angharad N. Valdivia, *Latina/os and the Media* (Malden, MA: Polity, 2010), 89.

16 Angharad N. Valdivia, *Latina/os and the Media* (Malden, MA: Polity, 2010), 89.

4

NOSTALGIA VERSUS
HISTORICAL CONTINUITY

Boston Rob, New York, and Imagining
Vulnerable Urban Identities

Boston Rob Mariano and Tiffany "New York" Pollard mark a unique phenomenon where reality contestants marry urban identities to ethnic or racial stereotypes to become successful reality gamers and lasting station personalities. In 2002, when Rob Mariano appeared on the fourth season of CBS's *Survivor* (2000–present), no one had ever come back for a second season, let alone moved on to another CBS reality show. But his thick Boston accent, white ethnic markers, and predilection for quoting *The Godfather* (1972) resulted in CBS casting him on three additional seasons of *Survivor*, two seasons of *The Amazing Race* (2001–present), and a wedding special for his marriage to fellow *Survivor* Amber Brkich. By the end of Rob's first season of *Survivor*, Jeff Probst and other contestants had already started calling him Boston Rob. He was known for his gangster- and trickster-like gaming. Something about Rob's ethnic performances spoke to the way CBS envisioned its brand, and Rob typically delivered an entertaining season, making it to the final episode in two seasons of *Survivor* and one season of *The Amazing Race*. Four years after Mariano launched the first successful reality gaming career, Tiffany Pollard repeated history on a different channel and through a different stereotype. She appeared on the first season of *Flavor of*

Love (2006–08) and made it to the final two by playing the role of the sapphire, a figure that Marilyn Yarborough and Crystal Bennett argue makes black women evil, rude, loud, malicious, and overbearing.[1] VH1 executives brought her back for Season Two of Flavor of Love (she again made it to the final two) and then gave her three of her own shows: I Love New York (2007–08), which ran for three seasons, New York Goes to Hollywood (2008), and New York Goes to Work (2009). Mariano and Pollard show that while a successful career as a reality gamer is possible, it is rare and usually results in the contestant competing in programs on the same channel.

In some ways, this chapter continues a theme from the previous chapter by examining the way reality television represents the financially vulnerable within America's global cities in order to win our consent for the political economy of social expulsions, but it differs crucially in three ways. First, the gamers willingly perform stereotypes of economically disempowered groups who were envisioned more for their long-term residency in cities and less for their ability to serve the elite. Second, Boston Rob and New York stand for entire cities. They function as what Rob Shields calls "place images" by reducing a complex urban space to one or two defining characteristics.[2] By doing this, Mariano and Pollard make those cities visible, whereas the servants and servers on Bravo programs often exist in spaces unseen by the elite. Third, Mariano and Pollard stand for cities in locales that are removed from society in order to construct gaming spaces that run by a different set of rules than those in society. John Bale calls such areas "third spaces," zones in between two established spaces where rules and identities are malleable.[3] The spaces of Survivor and other CBS game shows are not Boston, but they are also not really the specific locales where the programs are shot. Contestants on Survivor: Borneo (2000) don't follow the laws of Borneo. They adhere to the rules of the game. These third spaces become experimental grounds to see what type of American identities can survive in a Darwinian world. Thus, on CBS reality programs, Rob Mariano allows viewers to evaluate how historically situated working-class, Italian American urban identities stack up against other versions of Americanness. Likewise, although Flavor of Love is filmed in a Los Angeles mansion, the space is removed from Los Angeles society and allows women of different races and classes to express their love for a hip hop icon. New York's stereotypical behavior is coded as ghetto. She stands for a type of urban black poverty amidst a diverse set of women.

The ethnic and racial urban identities that Mariano and Pollard perform are examples of the way scholars theorize identities on reality television as both excessive and reductive. In this chapter I use the term *amplify* to address the way contestants perform identities. The dictionary definition of *amplify* is "to increase the strength of. To make louder by increasing the strength of signals."[4] Contestants amplify identities when they make one part incredibly loud and other parts silent. They amplify one note on an identity's full musical scale in order to make the identity just that one note. My use of the term resonates with the ways scholars address the magnification of identity characteristics on reality television. Misha Kavka argues that reality contestants "flaunt" their identities, a term that connotes a camp form of showing off and one-upping others.[5] Theri A. Pickens explores how identities are ratcheted on reality television, a strategy whereby a contestant moves notch-by-notch from the realm of the respectable normality to stereotypical outlandishness.[6] Like flaunting and ratcheting, amplifying exaggerates a few identity traits and ignores others. I have chosen to add amplify to the mix of critical terms for identity on reality television, since flaunting—tied to camp—has a gender-specific basis, and ratcheting—given the stereotype of the black ratchet—comes with a specific focus on black femininity. Amplifying is more of a neutral term that can accommodate various identities. It allows me to speak about flamboyant performances without co-opting a critical term for a specific identity group.

Amplifying urban identities worked well for Mariano and Pollard because it made them good strategists in the game and good figures for the station brand, creating a mutually advantageous relationship between the contestant and the channel. The channel aired reality games where an amplified ethnic or racial identity could form the basis of a successful gaming strategy. Strategizing as a gangster or a trickster got Rob to the final episode half of the times he played a CBS reality game show. As a sapphire, New York made it to the finals 100 percent of the time. But these figures also allowed the stations to create reality programs that fit the channel brand. CBS engaged in a rebrand in the early 2000s in an effort to become the number one network in America by offering quality cinematic programming, and *Survivor* was a crucial part of the rebrand through the way it offered movie-like aesthetics and a thinking-person's game. The emphasis was on the character's strategic moves, not the character's backstory, so Rob's stereotypical Italian American identities made him an instantly recognizable figure and formed the foundation for good game playing strategies. VH1 was also in the midst of a rebrand in the mid-2000s, transforming itself from nostalgic channel that viewed popular culture's past as ironic to a channel that developed its own contemporary campy reality stars. New York first appeared on a show nostalgically recalling Flavor Flav as a figure from the 1980s, but her flamboyance and sapphire-like behavior became part of a theatrical approach toward life on the channel and made her VH1's first homegrown reality star.

Despite being united through a shared phenomenon, Boston Rob and New York show the ways that different racial and ethnic groups can be used to win the consent for the political economy of social expulsions. White working-class neighborhoods are increasingly disappearing in the era of social expulsions. Rob's popularity as a CBS reality persona speaks to a nostalgic vision of urban life. CBS reality programs use this figure of the working-class ethnic sincerely, winning our approval of the contemporary economy by imagining that global cities still accommodate this vulnerable white social group. New York's stereotypical identity registers historical continuity. New York helped make VH1 programming focus more on the now than on the past, and her success speaks to how the poor African American is a figure from the past who still occupies today's global cities. The way shows with New York frame her ironically reveals how subconscious racism can also be mobilized to win consent—as African American economic abjection becomes something that we find humorous in America's global cities.

BOSTON ROB'S GAMEPLAY: HOW ETHNIC URBAN NOSTALGIA BECAME PART OF CBS'S QUEST TO BECOME AMERICA'S NUMBER ONE CHANNEL THROUGH QUALITY PROGRAMMING

The working-class figure of the Italian American urbanite is a myth that cities like to hold onto in the era of urban expulsions. Steve Puleo argues that Little Italies surfaced in American cities between 1880 and 1921 when more than 4.2 million Italians immigrated to the United States. These neighborhoods became close-knit, poor, and working-class ethnic enclaves that "acted as buffer zones of comfort and familiarity in the midst of a strange and hostile urban landscape."[7] In Boston these neighborhoods popped up in East Boston and the North End. The neighborhoods became diluted through two separate historical events. First, post-World War II Boston witnessed many Italian Americans rise in social class and move to commuting towns such as Chelsea, Quincy, Malden, and Medford.[8] But for the people who stayed in Boston's Little Italies, life became increasingly untenable near the end of the century. Many Italian neighborhoods remained poor but witnessed a Latino influx. Others became gentrified and were no longer affordable to working-class Italian Americans. As a result, Italians now make up fewer than 10 percent of Boston's population. Still, Puleo argues that many North End neighborhoods retain an Italian flare through the way Italian restaurants mark ethnic history. These eateries help a tourist industry nostalgically remember early twentieth-century Boston.

Boston Rob also becomes a myth of older ethnic urbanity. Mariano talks with a thick Boston accent, has dark skin and black hair that instantly mark him as Italian, and wears baseball caps for Boston sports teams (a Patriots cap in his first season of *Survivor* and a Red Sox cap in subsequent seasons). Season Four of *Survivor* initially billed Mariano as coming from Canton, Massachusetts, a town twenty miles south of Boston that became a popular destination for Italians in the postwar era. But over the course of Season Four, Rob became known as Boston Rob, which clearly defined him as an early twentieth-century urbanite.

Boston Rob offers a cultural nostalgia for older ways of urban life through a process that I term the *imagination of expulsions*. One way neoliberal urbanism works is by retaining one-dimensional images of groups recently expelled from areas to make them seem still central to the area. For example, Daniel Rosensweig's study of Jacobs Field in Cleveland shows how developers seized land from a poor neighborhood and displaced many African American renters, homeowners, and homeless people in order to build a highly policed ballpark that would bring in wealthy white spectators and keep poor African Americans at bay. At the same time, the stadium designers built memorials to African American athletes to create a safe and sanitized version of blackness available to white patrons.[9] Christopher Mele's study of lower Manhattan in the 1980s shows how SoHo and the East Village expelled artists and punk rock musicians once central to the area, but then designed buildings with the same counter-cultural aesthetic to appeal to upper-class whites moving to the area.[10] Working-class, poor, minority, and alternative identities become commodified and sanitized for financially successful whites, a strategy that lets new residents consume former identities without interacting with these social classes.

Boston Rob's place within the imagination of expulsions is unique, for his identity is held up as central in a third space, not within the area from which he was expelled. Instead of finding alternative ways to visualize a population no longer in a city, here the imagination asks the older urban identity to make a claim to relevance within a larger imagined space depicting America and operating by a different set of social rules. Thus, on *Survivor*, Boston Rob no longer makes the working-class ethnic relevant just to Boston; he makes the Bostonian working-class ethnic essential to America.

The America to which Rob seems central on *Survivor* is not a reflection of the country but an experiment with its citizens. On early seasons of *Survivor*, host Jeff Probst often spoke of the program as a social experiment, a premise that shapes reality on some reality television programs. Media scholar Anna McCarthy traces the social experimental nature of reality television back to *Candid Camera* (1948–67, first run). Allen Funt used the language of post-World War II social science to create social experiments that measured people's responses when certain elements were changed.[11] For example, the "Allen Rides in a Trunk" skit tests people's reaction to a couple driving in a car to see how they react when the man is locked in the trunk. The changed variable on *Survivor* is the space that social groups inhabit. Whereas real life separates social groups in space through geographies of economic and social power, *Survivor* brings them together to inhabit the same space. It tests which social identities are best suited to thrive in a social Darwinist gaming world stripped of modern conveniences and reliant on people providing life's basics—food, water, fire, and shelter—for themselves. For example, a medical doctor has more cultural, social, and economic capital than a truck driver, but Season One of *Survivor* put people from these two backgrounds into the game. Truck driver Sue Hawk made it to the final four based on her social skills, gaming strategy, and physical play, while the medical doctor, Sean Kniff, was eliminated early in the season because of his naïve strategizing. Some seasons have divided tribes along social divisions. Season Thirty broke teams into class divisions—white-collar, blue-collar, and no-collar—and blue-collar contestant Mike won. In the case of Boston Rob, *Survivor* offers an alternative universe to Boston itself. While real cities made life for blue-collar Italian Americans increasingly untenable, *Survivor* allows them to thrive in an alternative society controlled not by brutal economic power but by gaming strategy. *Survivor* offers the opportunity for people with marginal identities to establish themselves as central in a controlled version of society, but the pleasure of *Survivor* is that a range of social identities compete for relevance. For every cop or construction worker who has won, a business owner or lawyer has as well.

The world of *Survivor* is set up to celebrate Italian American stereotypes, which is why Boston Rob is arguably the most memorable contestant. *Survivor* differs from the gaming space in *The Amazing Race* where contestants can win if they try hard and eliminate interpersonal conflict. *Survivor* favors duplicity over meritocracy. Its motto is "Outwit. Outplay. Outlast." Outwitting involves blindsides, a common move in the game, where contestants must lure a cast member into a false sense of security and then vote him or her off. Social strategy within the game constantly involves lying to people to gain advantages at tribal council. Moreover, the game is full of advantages that give the upper hand to some contestants. Reward challenges sometimes offer food; the nourished competitor has a distinct advantage over the other starving cast members at immunity challenges. Part of the pleasure of *Survivor* is seeing how unfair advantages and secret scheming affect the game. Boston Rob worked so well on *Survivor* because the stereotypes he performed were based on the same values that *Survivor* prized: deception, manipulation, and scheming. Boston Rob could bring to life ethnic stereotypes and advance within the game at the same time.

Boston Rob is a product of the imagination of expulsions through the way he is able to reduce Italian American identity to one trait, shifty gaming, in order to make it seem like this ethnicity still occupies a crucial role in Boston. On *Survivor*, Rob Mariano stands for older ethnic urbanisms through the historical stereotypes he performs, the gangster and the trickster, that emerged from a moment when Little Italies flourished in cities. Jonathan Cavallero argues both stereotypes surfaced in the 1930s in response to the first wave of Italian immigration and in an effort to enforce nativism as a way to demonize Italian immigrants as American job stealers. But the stereotypes also surfaced during the Great Depression, one of capitalism's greatest failures. The gangster and trickster stereotypes had different relationships to the feasibility of the American Dream and the fallibility of the economic system at this time. The gangster pursues the American Dream of class mobility but does so through sinful means in order to achieve gluttonous results. The gangster's corruption of the American Dream becomes a way to blame ethnicity for economic failures and refuses to interrogate the economic system itself as a source of injustice. The Italian American gangsters found in 1930s films such as Little Caesar (1931) and Scarface (1932) were all city boys. As a gangster, Rob corrupts the democratic nature of the game in an attempt to make it more of a dictatorship as he tries to rise in class through winning the million dollars. The Italian American trickster, however, is able to point out how the entire socio-economic system is corrupt and then take advantage of it in humorous ways for personal gains. The Italian American trickster sees the self-centered nature of all of those surrounding him or her, and the trickster succeeds by exploiting this human trait for personal gain. The manipulative and disloyal nature of the trickster is not demonized or used as a cautionary tale. It is lionized in a world where traditional values would lead only to failure.[12] When Rob plays as a trickster, he constructs seemingly collaborative relationships in the game and then humorously backstabs people.

Rob brings these historically situated Italian American stereotypes to screen by making them the driving logic of his gaming strategy. Rob strategizes like a gangster in Seasons Four, Twenty, and Twenty-two. In the third episode, "No Pain, No Gain," of Season Four Rob explains in a confessional how his strategy is indebted to the movie The Godfather. The episode requires the first big game move of the season. Although Rob's tribe, Maramu, went to tribal in the previous two episodes, the decisions on who to vote out were obvious. The tribe first voted out a male hippie with awkward social skills and then an older, out-of-shape woman who struggled in challenges. The immunity challenge loss in this third episode has most members of

Figure 4.1 A cunning Boston Rob Mariano on the fourth season of *Survivor*.
CBS/Photofest ©CBS

Maramu wanting to vote out lazy Sarah, but Rob targets Hunter, the strongest person on the tribe. Rob explains:

> It is important for me to have people on my team able to do what I tell them to do and not know that I'm telling them to do that. It doesn't matter if my team is stronger physically or even stronger mentally. But just that they obey. It's all in how smart these people are. If they realize that they need you that is what will keep them loyal. Right? Fear. Basically, it's a tough principal. But fear keeps people loyal. If they are afraid, they have something to lose. Then they will do what you tell them to do. That's straight out of *The Godfather*.

When Rob plays up his gangster heritage, he bullies his tribe members to follow him and purposefully takes the role of leader to minimize the need for other tribe members to strategize with each other. Notice the corruption of democracy in Rob's move. The tribe collectively wants to eliminate the person who is least committed to helping them win, but Rob manipulates all of them to vote out the person least likely to obey him. These gangster actions failed to gain momentum on Season Four because a redrawing of the tribes in Episode Four put Rob in a new tribe where Maramu was outnumbered four to three and led to his elimination by Episode Seven. But that same strategy won him the million dollars on Season Twenty-two and put him in a good position to win Season Twenty.

The most sinful example of the gangster's moves corrupting the game appears in the final tribal council of Season Twenty-two when Boston Rob wins the million dollars unanimously. Rob brought two competitors with him who were completely undeserving of the million dollars: Natalie, a college student who lacked self-confidence, and Phillip, who straddled the line between socially awkward and mentally ill. He wore only pink bikini briefs throughout the season, talked about his stealth mode strategy (which no one followed), and often spoke—in completely insincere and comical terms—about how his time on Survivor was fueled by his Native American heritage. Rob strategically orchestrated the eliminations so that the least deserving people remained with him at the final tribal council. During their opening statements to the jury, the only case that Natalie and Phillip make to the jury about why they made it to the end is that they aligned with Boston Rob. Rob, however, explains how many challenges he won, how he worked hard at camp, and how he had to make and break alliances to win the game. The final tribal council is a true corruption of the game to its fans. Phillip is so mentally unstable that he gets into emotionally volatile fights when anyone asks him a question, and Natalie does not have the skills to position herself as a viable candidate with confidence. Rob's manipulation of the game made the tribal council a formality, as no one could vote for the other candidates.

Rob employs his other strategy in Season Eight, the first all-stars season, when he plays the role of the stereotypical Italian American trickster who seemingly works with others in a collaborative environment and then proceeds to back stab people. In this season, Rob is an artful, silly con.

The shift makes Rob much more likeable because corruption in the game moves from Rob's elimination of competition in general to Rob's taking advantage of everyone else's greed and hypocrisy. For example, Lex from *Survivor: Africa* is a narcissist on the Mogo Mogo tribe who likes to hear himself talk about how friendships matter to him but how he would never place friendship over the business of winning the game. Whenever Lex plays a key role in voting off friends, he talks to them alone and delivers a self-congratulatory speech about how he values them as people; voting them off is simply his game strategy.

Whereas other players fell victim to Lex, Rob exploited Lex's narcissism at a crucial point. Jeff Probst attempts to redraw the tribes in the tenth episode, "Mad Scramble and Broken Hearts," by having contestants pick a new team bandana from a vase. Everyone except Amber swaps tribes, meaning the former Mogo Mogo is now Chapera with Amber on it. This devastates Rob, who has made a sincere alliance with Amber and has romantic feelings for her. When Chapera loses the immunity challenge in the episode, Rob pulls Lex aside as the tribes are walking away and says, "You take care of her (Amber), and I'll take care of you." In what is one of the all-time dumbest moves in *Survivor*, Lex gets his tribe to vote off Jerri to save Amber. This defies common sense, as voting off Amber would have made the tribes have the same numbers at the merge. Rob's trickery succeeds because he comes across as so sincere in his plea to Lex, and Lex is so caught up in his own sincerity that he sees himself in Rob. After the merge occurs in the next episode, Rob immediately votes off Lex and laughs in numerous confessionals about how stupid Lex was to believe him.

The season that portrays Rob as a trickster showcases Rob's humor more than his gangster seasons do. This comes through in Rob's own thoughts on his fellow cast members. In the fourteenth episode, "A Chapera Surprise," family members visit the remaining contestants. Rob recounts the Lex event to his brother. Smiling, Rob says, "I was like, Lex, do me a favor. Keep the girl, and I'll help you out on the reverse side. Alright, so the dumbass actually kept her, and then I snaked him," while Rob's brother doubles over in laughter. Later in the episode, Rob reflects on what it was like to meet fellow tribe member Big Tom's son, claiming, "Bo's a bigger dumbass than his dad. I mean, Big Tom is pretty dumb, but Bo is just, he's out there, too."

Rob also performs his trickster ethnicity when he and Amber compete on Season Seven of *The Amazing Race* shortly after their marriage. For example, the "Mow 'em Down Like Grass" episode is set in Jaipur, India. Rob reworks the game structure whereby competitions are level playing fields that introduce contestants to local cultures when he convinces Sanjay, a local hotel manager, to help them in the competitions in his city. Producers gave contestants a monetary allowance for transportation. Rob was the first and only contestant to use it to hire locals for a competitive advantage in the game, although Sanjay turned down Rob's offer and helped for free. With Sanjay's help, Rob maneuvers through the city faster than his competitors. At this point in the season Rob and Amber have an alliance with Ron and Kelly, and Rob artfully tells Sanjay that if a situation arises where he and Amber have to beat Ron and Kelly, Sanjay should stick with Rob and Amber. Throughout the season Rob instructs travel agents helping him book flights not to give the earliest flight options to other teams so Rob and Amber can gain an advantage.

The way Rob is portrayed through the imagination of expulsions means that Italian American identities are used in a celebratory manner to win our consent for the current political economy. The fact that Rob performs two Italian American stereotypes on CBS reality shows should not be understood as CBS somehow mocking this ethnic group. The imagination of expulsions, in fact, shares the same mode of identity construction that stereotyping does. It takes complex identities and reduces them to one or two traits, but it does this in order to mask a social eviction and redeem a group as still central to a space. The question, then, becomes why CBS executives would find remembering residual Italian American urban identities important.

The residual Italian American identities that Boston Rob embodied offered CBS a useful reservoir of ethnic images for its quality brand. The shifty nature of gangsters and tricksters provided different ways to perceive reality that fit well with CBS's construction of reality as a game. By relying on stereotypes that Rob Mariano performed, CBS was able to highlight Rob's contribution to the narratives of *Survivor* and *The Amazing Race* and give only a superficial backstory of him—only that he worked in construction and was a blue-collar ethnic from Boston. This allowed *Survivor* and *The Amazing Race* to dedicate less time to character development and more time to game strategies. Such a strategy highlighted the intellectual labor of a contestant for a network constructing a quality brand.

In the early 2000s, CBS President Les Moonves engaged in a significant rebrand of CBS and billed it as a quality network and America's number one network. The grandiosity of the channel identity is partly the result of branding a network channel instead of a cable channel. Whereas MTV could just brand itself as a youth channel or ESPN could target sports viewers, CBS still had to draw in a larger constituency of viewers. Rather than craft a specific identity for a target audience, CBS attempted to mark itself simply as the best through the way it discussed its quality programming. As Michael Z. Newman and Elana Levine argue, twenty-first-century American culture legitimizes television as a medium of value and sophistication.[13] Perhaps the biggest way that CBS branded itself as an elite network is through the way it created a lineup to take away Thursday night ratings from NBC, which had dwarfed the other networks with its must-see-TV line up in the 1980s and 1990s. Moonves has consistently billed his network's overthrow of NBC on Thursday night as a triumph of quality. In 2010 he said:

> Remember, NBC was invincible on Thursday night. It was a case where I thought we never could attack them head on. But then we could because of *Survivor* and *CSI*. It would have gone there anyway with or without *Survivor*. There are bad versions of everything, but watching this last group [of contestants], the quality of the show is still there. *Survivor* is a class act.[14]

Elsewhere Moonves has grouped *Everyone Loves Raymond* in with his quality Thursday night programs.[15] Moonves' statements reveal that promotional discourses about quality often trump textual features, as *Everyone Loves Raymond* is a classic multicam sitcom that Newman and Levine identify as more middlebrow than the sophisticated single-cam comedies, and *CSI* lacks the textured characters and nuanced plot details that Jason Mittell argues constitute complex TV drama.[16]

Moonves and other CBS executives carefully claimed *Survivor* as part of CBS' quality line up but also distanced the network from trends in reality television. For example, in 2003 Moonves said, "There's a reason there's going to be a seventh and eighth *Survivor* this year. Somehow, I don't think you'll see a seventh *Are You Hot?*"[17] In 2009 CBS Entertainment president Nina Tassler offered this reflection upon *Survivor* being renewed for its nineteenth and twentieth seasons: "*Survivor* is one of CBS' signature series and a symbol of enduring quality and entertainment on primetime television."[18] These comments demonstrate genres themselves function as discourses to be used by speakers for social and political purposes.[19] Although it is commonly understood that *Survivor* started the twenty-first-century boom in reality television, CBS executives routinely claim the show to be in a larger category of quality television and actively avoid labelling it as reality television. The executives reinforced a larger cultural trend that Brenda Weber identifies: the tendency to view reality television as trash and the very worst form of TV.[20] Sometimes executives and reality producers partly legitimized CBS reality shows as quality television by stressing the shows' connections to sophisticated cinema. Warner Bros. Television president Peter Roth said that film producer Jerry Bruckheimer elevated the visual style of CBS programming by making scripted series such as *CSI: Crime Scene Investigation* (2000–13), *Cold Case* (2003–10), and *Without a Trace* (2002–09) and reality programs such as *The Amazing Race*. Roth claimed Bruckheimer "raised the viewers' expectations by introducing a motion-picture look to TV."[21] Other times, executives focussed on the budgets of reality shows and how they were more in line with the financing of quality dramas. Moonves said that CBS invests an unusually high amount of money in the production costs of signature reality series, noting that, in 2010, *Survivor* costs more per episode than a new television drama would, which adds up to 2.3 million dollars per episode.[22] These examples show how CBS discursively constructed *Survivor* as both a reality program and something more than a reality program.

Gaming became a key textual feature of *Survivor* that helped to contribute to CBS's quality brand, and the program's ability to reduce character traits to one or two items allowed *Survivor* to spend more time on the intellectual nature of gaming. Instead of learning about what makes Rob Mariano a complex person, the show, after identifying him as a Boston Italian, can focus on who Rob chooses to align with, who they choose to eliminate, who they choose to blindside, how they handle rewards, how they play idols, etc. All of this highlights strategy and distinguishes the reality game show from the reality competition show. When *The Bachelor* has a group of women compete to win the heart of a man or *American Idol* (2002–16) has singers compete for the title of best singer, these shows have contestants use some type of talent—in this case looks or artistry—to win over someone else, be it a potential spouse or a judge. But *Survivor* focuses on the cerebral aspects of outplaying your competitors, of outsmarting them with better game play. One-dimensional characters such as Rob help make *Survivor* a show about strategy, not character.

Thus, Rob's emergence as the most frequently cast *Survivor* contestant is a case where his amplified identity resonates with culture and industry. On *Survivor* Rob speaks to a larger imagination of expulsions whereby Americans envision expelled social groups as central to urban space. And as CBS works to create a brand that includes reality television as quality programming, Rob's performance of ethnic stereotypes is a way to enact cerebral gaming strategies.

NEW YORK AS SAPPHIRE: THE PERSISTENCE OF THE BLACK GHETTO IN CONTEMPORARY CITIES AND ITS PLACE IN VH1'S EVOLVING BRAND

Rob Mariano is a figure that appeals to our longings for past urbanisms, but Tiffany Pollard is a contemporary figure, to the extent that VH1's desire to have New York represent urban black ghetto life was a desire to have her represent an aspect of city life that is still part of global capitalist cities. As Saskia Sassen argues, global cities are now centers for extreme wealth and extreme poverty. John Charles Boger and Judith Welch Wegner argue that, since 1980, urban poverty has been concentrated in black and Hispanic neighborhoods.[23] Tiffany Pollard's performance of the black sapphire stereotype was hardly, in and of itself, unique to the way African American women appear on reality television. Jervette R. Ward, Sheena Harris, and LaToya Jefferson-James argue that reality television often reduces the complex lives of African American women to the angry black woman figure.[24] Ward argues the sapphire image surfaced through the white imagination as a way to create intra-social group conflict. But as Pickens argues, such flamboyant behaviors, typically coded in offensive ways as "ghetto," become a way to chart individual careers through reality television, even though these behaviors violate the respectability of African Americans.[25]

What makes Pollard unique is how she merges this figure to a specific city to show the persistence of urban black economic abjection. Black ghettoes in northeastern cities, such as New York, emerged as safe spaces before the end of the Civil War, a place where African Americans could live after fleeing slavery in the South by way of the Underground Railroad. Additionally, many African Americans migrated to poor black neighborhoods in Northeastern cities after slavery to escape the racist legacy of the South. As Boger and Wegner show, black poverty remains in contemporary cities in ways that white working-class ethnics do not.

Tiffany Pollard stood for New York City grittiness and ghetto life on VH1, even though she isn't even from New York City. She is from Syracuse, New York, and got her name not because she pretended to be from New York City. Flav gives all women on the show hip hop nicknames to use all season. They are never referred to by their birth names. New York is an interesting name for a locale, for it can refer either to New York City or New York State. The slippage is evident in the city's sports teams, all of which simply go by New York, not New York City. The premiere episode, "Fifteen Beds and a Bucket of Puke," shows how VH1 wanted to play on this slippage and bill Pollard as an urban-based sapphire who has the grit and personality of America's largest city. Flavor conducts a naming ceremony where he asks the women about themselves, and he gives them an appropriate name. New York is noticeably not shown during the ceremony, even though she is clearly the co-star of the show. One can assume this is because she either says she is from Syracuse or New York State. This omission allows all of New York's sapphire performances to become coded as New York City ghetto behavior.

What emerges through this slippage, though, is an image of New York City that is larger than life. After all, Flavor Flav is an iconic New York City rapper known for his flamboyant styles. His fashion stood out in Public Enemy where lead rapper Chuck D wore subdued working-class outfits of jeans, t-shirts, and a baseball caps. Often other members wore the iconic berets of the nationalist group The Black Panthers. But Flavor dressed in ornate urban outfits—huge clocks around his neck, top hats, sunglasses, flamboyant coats, etc. Flavor Flav's over-the-top style assisted him as the hype man for one of the most socially conscious rap groups of all time. The group addressed systemic racism, the legacy of slavery, the failure of the police force and emergency medical system to keep black neighborhoods safe, and Arizona's racist decision not to celebrate Martin Luther King, Jr., Day. As hype man, Flavor's job was to bring an energy to the group's music and performance, and his extravagant outfits helped with that. New York is equally as over the top. She wears gigantic fake eyelashes. She speaks in an exaggerated way, often slowing her speech to make a point, flipping her hair during conversation, and rising on her tippy toes during a fight. She is often loud. Her appearance is so over the top that women on the show call her a drag queen. She and Flav are the most flamboyant people on the show.

Because the competition of *Flavor of Love* is performed in a third space (it takes place in a Los Angeles mansion, and contestants cannot leave unless there is a reward challenge or they are eliminated), black poverty appears visually through a set of performed characteristics, not through a venture into actual poor black neighborhoods in real cities. When Pickens explains the ratchet (a modern term for sapphire) combines ghetto behavior with a "hot shitty mess" attitude, the implication is that the ghetto surfaces through a combination of diva-like behavior (screaming, eye rolling, hair flipping, volatility, etc.), over-the-top urban fashion, and an extravagant use of beauty products.

Performing these coded urban ghetto traits becomes New York's strategy to advance in the competition of *Flavor of Love* Seasons One and Two. She uses the traits partly to shock her competition so that they focus on fighting with her and not pursuing Flavor Flav. This first appears in the second episode of Season One titled "Rub a Dub Flav." The episode opens with the women eating breakfast and reading a card, known as a Flav-O-Gram, from Flav that says today there will be a hot tub challenge where each woman will have ten minutes alone with Flav in a hot tub. The three who leave the biggest impression will receive more time with the rapper. Every woman remaining in the competition is at breakfast except New York, who comes down shortly after the Flav-O-Gram is read. New York's entrance is theatrical. With over-the-top fakeness, she looks at every contestant individually, waves, and says hi with forced sweetness. When she gets to Rain, she dramatically whips her arm, tosses her hair to the side, points, and says, "Not you. You can choke." The scene cuts to a confessional of New York, who says in a very clinical, emotionless, and slightly sociopathic way, "This is the first interaction I really had with Rain, so I wanted to see her, ah, her anger level. I wanted to see if I was powerful enough to twist her mind." The episode lets viewers know that New York is that powerful. While the women drive in a van to the resort with a hot tub, Goldie asks New York what she would do if Flav had nothing on in the hot tub. Angering the other women, New York looks disgusted and says, "Well, I just have a lot on my mind right now, and I don't feel like talking." When Pumkin tells New York she has the opportunity to make friends with a lot of women in the house, New York says, "Yeah, I do, but I don't want to take the opportunity." A screaming match ensues between New York and Rain about how the women should act. Once at the resort, Rain is still bothered by the fight, but New York takes her time in the hot tub to tell Flav she is a peacemaker and the type of calming force Flav needs in his life. Although the sincerity that Flav sees contrasts with what viewers and other contestants know about her, she wins a slot in the three-contestant date with Flav the next day. Rain remains unfocussed during her time with Flavor Flav, and her failure to make an impression results in her being eliminated.

New York balances her angry black woman aggression to the other women with her sincerity with Flav by performing an obviously phony, exaggerated kindness when she is with the women and Flav at the same time, a strategy that both angers the women and charms Flav. For example, Flavor Flav takes the women to Las Vegas in the fifth episode, "What Happens in Flavor Stays in Flavor," and gives them 100 dollars to use at a roulette table. All of the women look pretty focussed on playing roulette, but when New York steps up, she uses a phony sincerity with Flav that angers the women. She tells him she needs to warm up before she plays and then grinds her backside against him in a flirtatious manner. After every winning move, she makes exaggerated, slow, joyous moves against Flav's body that contrast with the aggression the women typically deal with from her. The scene edits in the other women looking disgusted, but New York continues with the same over-the-top kindness toward the other competitors that she has toward Flav. She tells them she is doing so well because her third eye sees all, and she blows kisses to the women in between plays. But it is exactly these types of performances in front of Flav and the women that win Flav's heart and channel the women's attention away from Flav and onto her. Because women focus their attention on New York instead of Flav, New York is able to advance to the final two in both seasons on the show.

New York was able to parlay her performance on *Flavor of Love* into a three-year reality career on VH1 because the way she competed as a sapphire resonated powerfully with the branding initiatives at the channel. When *Flavor of Love* began in 2006, VH1 had an interest in creating shows around larger-than-life kitschy celebrities from the 1970s, 1980s, and 1990s. VH1 executives thought of these shows as ironic. VH1 had begun to take an ironic approach to popular culture with the 1996 premiere of *Pop Up Video* (1996–2002, first run), but history was not a focus on the show. The program had sarcastic pop-up captions appear on screen that made fun of contemporary and historical videos. VH1 was interested in the history of popular culture around the same time it created *Behind the Music* (1997–present) in 1997, a serious look at the rise and fall of musicians. In 2002, Brian Graden joined VH1's staff and worked with new VH1 president Christina Van Norman to turn VH1 into one of the most recognizable cable stations by merging the ironic focus of *Pop Up Video* with the nostalgia of *Behind the Music*. The channel would cast its eyes backward to laugh at the ridiculousness of popular culture's past. In the early 2000s VH1 created *I Love The 70s* (2003), *I Love The 80s* (2002), and *I Love The 90s* (2004) where a team of comedians mocked clips from key films, television shows, and music videos of one specific year.[26] Executives started VH1's "celebreality" programming in 2004 when they purchased *The Surreal Life* (2003–06) from the WB, where the program had aired for two seasons. The show took five, six, or seven stars who were iconic, kitschy figures from previous decades and placed them in a house together. *The Surreal Life* took a cynical "where are they now?" approach to stardom. Tom Calderone took over for Brian Graden in 2005 and developed original VH1 celebreality series that followed kitschy, instantly recognizable stars of the 1970s and 1980s in series such as *Hogan Knows Best* (2005–07), *Breaking Bonaduce* (2005–07), and *My Fair Brady* (2005–08). Calderone said his shows "have a certain quirkiness to [them], a certain sense of humor, a certain wink, wink, nudge, nudge that only VH1 can do (while) also not (taking) itself too seriously."[27] Dating shows about former iconic 1980s music artists such as *Flavor of Love* and *Rock of Love* (2007–09) with Brett Michaels were also part of this moment.

The "wink, wink" aspect of VH1's irony needs some further elaboration before we can understand the contradictory way that it displays race and poverty. The previous chapter dealt with Bravo's irony, which was when a character's actions conveyed the exact opposite of who they claimed to be. Recall Andy Cohen saying if someone said she was healthy, they would then edit in a shot of her smoking. The irony on VH1 is more stylized and incorporates elements of camp. As numerous scholars have noted, camp is a style based on artifice. Susan Sontag argues that "camp is a vision of the world in terms of style—but a particular kind of style. It is a love of the exaggerated, the off, of things-being-what-they-are-not."[28] The wink, wink approach to irony on VH1 is an aesthetic view of the world where popular culture's past offers an exaggerated vision of the world that takes us out of the realm of reality.

The racial politics of camp on *Flavor of Love* are contradictory; while the channel's camp can introduce black knowledge into typically white worlds, it frequently, and sometimes simultaneously, undercuts Flavor Flav's commitment to black economic justice by transforming poverty from something to eradicate to something at which to laugh. The frequent display of the mansion grounds on *Flavor of Love* demonstrates this. Visually the grounds resemble those of the mansion on ABC's *The Bachelor* (2002–present), the dating show on which *Flavor of Love* is based. But while *The Bachelor* predominantly casts white people and has never had an African American lead, *Flavor of Love* introduces a hyper-stylized blackness to the grounds and the mansion by decorating them with huge clocks. Flav has frequently said that within the visual imagery of Public Enemy, his clocks (he usually wears big ones around his neck) have symbolized the importance to take political action now. They add a temporal urgency to the Black Nationalist and anti-racist messages of Public Enemy. On *Flavor of Love*, these clocks are recast as a camp part of popular culture's past. They become part of a larger mise-en-scene that is seen through the channel's wink, wink lens. It's not just that there is one clock on the front lawn. The front lawn has huge dinosaur statues wearing Flavor Flav clocks and capes. The house stairwell is adorned with dozens of Flav clocks. The show transitions between day and evening scenes with exterior mansion shots with a CGI moon rising in a silly manner over the dinosaur decorated front lawn. While the camp aesthetics place black cultural markers into a mise-en-scene typically reserved for an all-white dating show, the way they merge the clocks with the general silliness of the dinosaurs robs them of the political message.

Something similar happens when we look at the campy nature of Flavor Flav's reward dinners on the show. In Public Enemy, Flavor Flav expressed his social commitments to end black economic poverty. On *Flavor of Love*, we see the reward dinners attempt to explore a different classed life outside of the exclusive mansion. This is a far cry from the world of *The Bachelor*, where all reward dates take place in elite parts of the city. *Flavor of Love* episodes feature a competition, such as who can cook the best soul food, who can babysit children the best, etc. Winners earn a private date with Flavor Flav where he takes them to a Los Angeles restaurant for dinner. The narratives of the reward dates mingle class codes for a laugh. The arcs begin with the

Figure 4.2 A publicity still for *Flavor of Love* shows how Flav's style fit with VH1's campy brand. Tiffany "New York" Pollard is in the front right of the picture.

VH1 Television/Photofest ©VH1 Television

woman wearing an ornate, high-fashion dress given to her by the producers. The winner stands at the top of the staircase of the mansion and waits for Flavor Flav to enter from the front door and take her to a limousine in the driveway. The show sets up viewers to think this is a high-class date, but the limousine always takes the couple to a restaurant with lower-class connotations, such as KFC, or with kitschy connotations, such as Medieval Times. The reward dinner at KFC includes numerous medium shots of Flavor Flav sloppily eating chicken. The scenes show in a camp manner an overly stylized approach to life, one showing life how it is not lived on *The Bachelor*, in order to venture into different classed spaces. But black poverty isn't shown as an economic condition; it's presented humorously through the messiness of Flavor Flav's eating habits and his complete lack of culture for choosing to eat at KFC.

New York capitalized on the campy irony in VH1's brand by amplifying the role of the sapphire to such an extent that her life on VH1 programs appeared to be lived in quotes, a camp expression used to describe performative exaggeration. New York's argument with Pumkin in the "Rub a Dub Flav" episode shows how New York bases her interpersonal skills on highly stylized, over-the-top behaviors. Their fight erupts late at night at the mansion when Pumkin confronts New York about her rudeness. This is the first time we see New York slow her speech and over-enunciate words to irritate people. When Pumkin says New York is ridiculous because she thinks she is going on a honeymoon with Flav, New York slowly screams, "I am. I am. I am. Yes, I am." With each I am, New York throws her head to a different side and elevates her height a little bit by standing more on her tippy toes. New York's insults are excessive and twist what others say. When Pumkin says she bets New York a million dollars she won't win, New York says "You don't have it, because if you did, you'd get a fucking face lift."

New York continued her campy insults on *I Love New York*, but she ironically inflected them on this series so that she would begin by sincerely complimenting a man and then move in to a camp insult-fest. Take her Season Two elimination of Frank "The Entertainer," a Long Islander who still lives in his parents' basement. At the elimination ceremony for an episode where Frank's parents visited the mansion and are still there at the ceremony, New York says:

Frank, you sure are the entertainer, because you keep me laughing, and you are so fun to be around. I've come to realize that it will never work between you and I. Frank, I'm on my way to the top, and you are still stuck in your parents' basement. I need a man who can support me and check me. And you don't even have the patience to mow the lawn right. With all due respect to you and your parents, you are a loser.

Figure 4.3 Tiffany "New York" Pollard. Her campy persona fit well with the VH1 brand.

VH1 Television/Photofest ©VH1 Television

This is exactly the type of camp that VH1 loved. She starts by sincerely exploring what made the two of them like each other, and then she amplifies her dislike through an exaggerated spatial metaphor (her rise to the top and Frank's descent into a basement) and a juvenile insult (calling him a loser in front of his parents.)

Part of the charm of the second season of I Love New York is that New York's rival love interests, Tailor Made and Buddha, allow New York to either amplify her camp approach to life or mute it. An African American man with the tall, muscular body of an NFL linebacker, Buddha brings out New York's sweet side through his calm, assertive personality. Her nickname for him shows how he presents a peaceful image. The series positions Buddha as a natural man. Much like The Buddha could transcend earthly miseries to achieve Nirvana, Buddha awakens New York to passions that focus her on intense love and divert her away from her explosive, campy behavior. Tailor Made, on the other hand, is a character based on artificiality. He is constructed, stitched together like his clothes. With his fondness for designer clothes and clean-cut hair, it is easy to read Tailor Made simply as a metrosexual. But that misses his over-the-top nature. It's not that Tailor Made wears designer clothes. It's that he parades them on a hanger through the house as he is looking for a place to change. It's that he often explains to the camera and contestants the greatness of the brands he is wearing. It's that he sleeps with his wardrobe next to him when the men in the house threaten his life. For Tailor Made, his wardrobe and his exterior are his life. Tailor Made cannot exist without them. New York also became associated with camp style, with her longer-than-you-could-imagine fake eyelashes, her extreme makeup that puts her one step removed from a clown, and her really long nails. As a small-framed, untoned white guy with a New York accent, Tailor Made indulges New York's excesses and welcomes her sapphire-like behavior. In the end, the second season of I Love New York celebrates camp when New York picks Tailor Made over Buddha.

Certainly, the camp aspects of New York's blackness do not undercut black politics the way VH1's camp presentation of Flavor Flav does; but at the same time, I Love New York presents black economic abjection as a series of stylized performances that make black urban poverty something to be enjoyed and laughed at. Black urban poverty emerges as a violation of middle-class norms. Translating black camp from *Flavor of Love* to *I Love New York* is dangerous; it negates the franchise's ability to attack *The Bachelor*'s racial exclusivity through Public Enemy imagery. Blackness no longer has the ambiguity of subverting white television norms through the iconography of a black rap group. Urban black life becomes nothing but a serious of outlandish performances, robbed of any progressive character.

The way Pollard stood for New York on VH1 is very different from the way Mariano stood for Boston on CBS, and while the differences are partly based on the way urban historical epochs frame the characters, it is also more than this and deals with how race and racism shape the way viewers are won over to accept the political economy of social expulsions. Rob is a fun character to watch, but there is a sincerity to the way that CBS portrays him. The nostalgia for which he stands is a serious one where we can genuinely imagine the contemporary city continuing to offer urban Italian American identities the way it did in the early twentieth century. But the tone of VH1's brand was based in campy irony, and although the channel wasn't overtly racist, the irony spilled over into laughing at black economic abjection. This says a lot about how viewer consent for the political economy of expulsions is mobilized. The black poverty that is still a crucial part of America's global cities becomes funny. This is a blunt form of consent winning that doesn't have to try hard and use the subtle negotiations that we have explored in previous chapters.

New York had a long career as a VH1 performer because her campy irony helped the channel move away from a focus on the ironies of popular culture's past and focus on the campiness of its own contemporary homegrown reality stars. She was the first regular contestant from a VH1 celebrity show to get her own show when *I Love New York* premiered on January 8, 2007. Then a new wave of programming emerged. Immediately following the April 15 finale of *I Love New York*'s Season One, *Flavor of Love: Charm School* (2007) premiered and offered the ironic premise of taking the uncouth women from Flavor Flav's series and training them to act like aristocratic women. The setting of a British training school coupled with the vulgar women offered a delightful irony. In 2009, VH1 took two contestants from *Rock of Love*, Daisy De La Hoya and Megan Hauserman, and gave them their own dating shows, *Daisy of Love* (2009) and *Megan Wants a Millionaire* (2009). Other shows that took contestants from VH1 reality series and placed them with new stars included I Love Money Seasons One (2008) and Two (2009), Real Chance at Love (2009), and Frank the Entertainer: A Basement Affair (2010).

Part of the way the VH1 carried on its camp reality programs was by casting eccentric people who lived life excessively, a practice that was destroyed when VH1 reality star Ryan Jenkins murdered his wife in 2009, fled to Canada, and committed suicide. Jenkins was a contestant on Megan Wants a Millionaire, which had aired three episodes at the time of the murder of Jasmine Fiore in Los Angeles on August 15, 2009. The finale of New York Goes to Work aired on June 29, 2009. There was a fairly abrupt sea change on VH1 after the Fiore murder. Jenkins had gone from Megan Wants a Millionaire to filming Season Three of I Love Money. VH1 never aired the rest of Megan Wants a Millionaire or the third season of I Love Money, which was set for a January 2010 premiere with Frank, The Entertainer: A Basement Affair. VH1 aired Frank's show but stopped its homegrown talent series immediately. Instead, it focussed on a more sober type of reality show featuring wives of African American athletes and musicians such as Basketball Wives (2010–13) and Love and Hip Hop (2011–present). Although these programs featured outlandish behavior, it was not as out-of-control as things were getting on VH1 homegrown reality series. VH1 added some respectability to their series by casting established professionals. This was an insurance policy. While wives might be dramatic, they had families with careers in entertainment and would not risk such monetary reward on violent crimes.

CONCLUSION

Boston Rob Mariano and Tiffany "New York" Pollard show another complex aspect of representing urban life on reality television in the age of social expulsions. Long-established urban ethnic and racial stereotypes become costumes for reality performances that led to long careers for these and other reality gamers. These performances spoke to deep-rooted assumptions about which economically disempowered social groups had a place in the contemporary city. Boston Rob appealed to viewer nostalgia for an older city. He called upon our desires to experience Little Italies that are losing significant demographic numbers but continue to exist through eateries. New York married the sapphire stereotype of the overbearing black woman with an urban ghetto geography in a way to call attention to the persistence of black disenfranchisement during the era of urban expulsions. African Americans still can exist in cities as the extremely poor. Rob wins our approval for the political economy of social expulsions through sentiment. New York does so through humor. There is one last way that reality television wins our consent for the exclusionary nature of America's global cities: the next chapter shows how rural shows offer either a temporary escape from the city or an affirmation of urban values.

NOTES

1 Marilyn Yarbrough and Crystal Bennett, "Cassandra and the Sistahs: The Peculiar Treatment of African American Women in the Myth of the Liars," *Journal of Gender, Race, and Justice* (Spring 2000), 626–57.

2 Rob Shields, *Places on the Margin: Alternative Geographies of Modernity* (New York: Routledge, 1991), 47.

3 John Bale, "Virtual Fandoms: Futurescapes of Football," in Adam Brown, ed., *Fanatics: Power, Identity, and Fandom in Football* (New York: Routledge, 1998), 265–78.

4 Amplify, Merriam-Webster Dictionary. Accessed August 8, 2016. http://www.merriam-webster.com/dictionary/amplify.

5 Misha Kavka, "Reality TV and the Gendered Politics of Flaunting," in Brenda Weber, ed., *Reality Gendervision: Sexuality and Gender on Transatlantic Reality Television* (Durham, NC: Duke University Press, 2014), 54–75.

6 Theri A. Pickens, "Shoving Aside the Politics of Respectability: Black Women, Reality Television, and the Ratchet," *Women & Performance: A Journal of Feminist Theory* (2014), 1–18.

7 Steve Puleo, *The Boston Italians: A Story of Pride, Perseverance, and Paesani, from the Years of the Great Immigration to the Present Day* (Boston, MA: Beacon, 2007).

8 Steve Puleo, *The Boston Italians: A Story of Pride, Perseverance, and Paesani, from the Years of the Great Immigration to the Present Day* (Boston, MA: Beacon, 2007), 226.

9 Daniel Rosensweig, *Retro Ball Parks: Instant History, Baseball, and the New American City* (Knoxville, TN: University of Tennessee, 2005), 113–42.

10 Christopher Mele, *Selling the Lower East Side: Culture, Real Estate, and Resistance in New York City* (Minneapolis, MN: University of Minnesota Press, 2004), 1–7.

11 Anna McCarthy, "Stanley Milgram, Allen Funt, and Me: Postwar Social Science and the 'First Wave' of Reality TV," in Susan Murray and Laurie Ouellette, eds, *Reality TV: Remaking Television Culture*, 1st edition (New York: New York University Press, 2004), 19–39.

12 Jonathan Cavallero, "Gangsters, Fessos, Tricksters, and Sopranos: The Historical Roots of Italian American Stereotype Anxiety," *Journal of Popular Film and Television* 32, no. 3 (June 2004), 50–63.

13 Michael Z. Newman and Elana Levine, *Legitimating Television: Media Convergence and Cultural Studies* (New York: Routledge, 2012), 1–14.

14 Rob Owen, "Survivor Marks 10 Years with Heroes-Villains Showdown," *Pittsburgh Post-Gazette*, February 11, 2010.

15 Alex Strachan, *The Gazette* (Montreal, QC), July 21, 2003.

16 Michael Z. Newman and Elana Levine, *Legitimating Television: Media Convergence and Cultural Studies* (New York: Routledge, 2012), 59–79; Jason Mittell, *Complex TV: The Poetics of Contemporary Television Storytelling* (New York: New York University Press, 2015).

17 Alex Strachan, *The Gazette* (Montreal, QC), July 21, 2003.

18 Neelie Andreeva, "Survivor Renewed for Two More Cycles," Hollywoodreporter. com, February 26, 2009.

19 James Naremore, *More Than Night: Film Noirs in Its Contexts* (Berkeley, CA: University of California Press, 1998); Rick Altman, *Film/Genre* (London: British Film Institute, 1999); Jason Mittell, *Genre and Television: From Cop Shows to Cartoons in American Culture* (New York: Routledge, 2004).

20 Brenda Weber, "Introduction: Trash Talk: Gender as an Analytic on Reality Television," in Brenda Weber, ed., *Reality Gendervision: Sexuality & Gender on Transatlantic Reality Television* (Durham, NC: Duke University Press, 2014), 1–34.

21 Chuck Barney, "Quality Networks' Theme: Stylized Shows with Intricate Character Development, Sprawling Plots Popular," *Wilkes Barre Times Leader*, August 23, 2006.

22 Rob Owen, "Survivor Marks 10 Years with Heroes-Villains Showdown," *Pittsburgh Post-Gazette*, February 11, 2010.

23 John Charles Boger and Judith Welch Wegener, eds, *Race, Poverty, and American Cities* (Chapel Hill, NC: University of North Carolina Press, 1996).

24 Jervette R. Ward, "The Real Scandal: Portrayals of Black Women in Reality TV," Scheena Harris, "Black Women: From Public Arena to Reality TV," and LaToya Jefferson-James, "Selective Reuptake: Perpetuating Misleading Cultural Identity in the Reality Television World," all in Jervette R. Ward, ed.,

Real Sister: Stereotypes, Respectability, and Black Women in Reality TV (New Brunswick, NJ: Rutgers University Press, 2015).

25 Theri A. Pickens, "Shoving Aside the Politics of Respectability: Black Women, Reality Television, and the Ratchet," *Women & Performance: A Journal of Feminist Theory* (2014), 3–5.

26 Craig Rosen, "It Was 20 Years Ago Today: Two Decades On, VH1 Has Changed Its Tune Several Times—But the Beat Goes On and On. (VH1 at 20)," *The Hollywoodreporter.com*, September 27, 2005. Accessed September 30, 2012.

27 Craig Rosen, "Music Man: New VH1 General Manager Tom Calderone Promises That Under His Watch, The Song Will Not Remain The Same," *The Hollywoodreporter.com*, September 27, 2005. Accessed September 30, 2012.

28 Susan Sontag, "Notes on Camp," in Fabio Cleto, ed., *Camp: Queer Aesthetics and the Performing Subject: A Reader* (Ann Arbor, MI: University of Michigan Press, 1999), 53.

5

GOLDEN AGES AND FOOL'S GOLD

Rural Reality Television during the Era of Urban Expulsions

At first it might seem counterintuitive, but rural reality shows play an important role in winning our consent for the political economy of social expulsions shaping America's global cities. Literary and cultural studies scholar Raymond Williams argues that the country and the city have a symbiotic relationship in fiction. This bond is particularly strong during moments of profound transformation in cities where, Williams argues, "the peace of country life could be contrasted with the . . . political chaos of cities."[1] While cities symbolize human achievement and are, thus, susceptible to human power struggles, the country frequently offers "a natural way of life: of peace, innocence, and simple virtue."[2] Although real country areas are caught in the midst of social, political, environmental, and economic conflict, fictive country spaces have a long history of existing as nostalgic spaces of tranquility. They show us more about what we imagine to be lacking in cities than what we actually find in the country. It's no surprise, then, that rural reality shows surface as the political economy of social expulsions transforms city life. Fictive country spaces serve as an ideal consent-winning vehicle, since they assure that crucial aspects of a good life that we desire in a city still exist; we just find them in the country now.

As we've seen in preceding chapters, reality television often draws on nostalgia to win viewers' approval for the political economy of social expulsions, mostly by placing residual urban identities either in contemporary cities or in third spaces (such as the gaming spaces on *Survivor* [2000–present]). Rural reality shows offer a unique way in which residual identities justify contemporary urban life. Rural reality shows construct a geographic space that remains apparently unaltered by time, where people who live in the country can remain there, untouched by the politics of social expulsions. But this escape from city spaces into nostalgic rural ones hardly offers a simple rejection of the urban. Rather it encourages an acceptance of contemporary city values.

There are two different forms of nostalgia on rural reality shows. The first represents the country as an Eden-like paradise stuck in a perpetual golden age. Shows in this tradition such as *Swamp People* (2010–present), *Moonshiners* (2011–present), *Alaska: The Last Frontier* (2011–present), and *Buying Alaska* (2012–15) fixate on the historical traditions of a rural region in order to show how these cultures and practices remain the same throughout the ages. Rural golden ages found in reality television support the political economy of expulsions by offering viewers a temporary escape from this brutality rather than a useful weapon to combat it. Shows such as *Here Comes Honey Boo Boo* (2012–14) offer an ironic lens to view the country whereby the derision of rural values on screen validates urban values off screen.

RURAL GOLDEN AGES

Looking at the past through the prism of a golden age privileges simplistic celebration over complex understanding. Williams argues the trope of the golden age is a way to critique the present, not grasp the past. The past comes to represent a stable and primitive community that humans often find lacking in their contemporary society. It's fitting that Western society often imagines golden ages through pastoral traditions, for the simplicity of the past coexists with the innocence of the country.[3] This simple look backward ignores the brutality of rural economics and industries. It is in this spirit that I examine how rural reality shows offer a golden age, but I do so by acknowledging that the way these programs engage history and nostalgia is tricky. Programs such as *Swamp People, Moonshiners,* and *Alaska: The Last Frontier* are obsessed with the minutia of history, so much so that they, at first, seem to trouble the notion that golden ages simplify history. The tiny details such as the hooks used to catch alligators and tools used to make illegal alcohol seem to create the types of reality shows made for history buffs. But a closer look reveals how the small details are used to reconstruct primitive communities, those in which humans had a lasting relationship with the land and that stand in stark contrast to the spaces of social expulsions.

Swamp People and *Moonshiners* use the same narrative strategy of editing in archival footage in between seasonal pursuits of contemporary rural residents to show how rural spaces are untainted by social progress. *Swamp People* follows several alligator hunters during the month-long alligator season in the Louisiana Swamps. Before the season, hunters purchase the right to kill a set number of alligators, represented by a tag. The seasonal arcs build on the tension of whether or not the hunters will catch an alligator for each tag. But each episode offers its own narrative tension as hunters go after a specific alligator who is legendary, a cannibal, or causing problems for human populations. Something as simple as setting a line to catch an alligator can spin off into a history lesson that uses archival footage. For example, "The Cannibal Gator" episode of *Swamp People* opens with Joe LaFont and his stepson Tommy hanging lines with barbed metal hooks and chicken meat from trees. The scene then cuts to a black-and-white image of two men at the end of a boat with a huge captured alligator between them. Then there is another black-and-white picture of a hunter with a dead alligator hanging over his shoulder. The narrator states, "Catching gators this way dates back to the early twentieth century." *Swamp People* often sets its sights on traditions that stretch back to the colonization of America, and the episode edits in sixteenth-century paintings of Native Americans hunting gators. The narrator says:

> But some of the first alligator hunters used a different method. In the sixteenth century Spanish explorers discovered that the Tahlequah Indians drove a sharpened tree trunk into the alligators mouth to flip it over, exposing the gator's soft underbelly for the kill.

The history lesson positions Joe and Tommy in a long line of regional alligator hunters. Cultural change is measured only through monumental epoch shifts, such as the transition from premodern indigenous hunting traditions to modern ones, in order to convey the longevity of traditions and the slowness of time.

The archival footage often bestows a primitivism on rural communities. This happens in the "Outlaw Brotherhood" episode of *Moonshiners* in Season One through the super 8 footage of legendary and now deceased moonshiner Marvin "Popcorn" Sutton. The Popcorn footage presents the long-lasting spiritual elements of moonshining in rural communities and contrasts it with the painstakingly precise brewing process of contemporary moonshiners. The step-by-step process of making moonshine narrated on the show threatens to rob the country of its simplicity. The episode begins with a twenty-minute segment of Tim Smith, the chief of Climax, Virginia's volunteer fire department, and his partner Tickle, two contemporary moonshiners, making a batch—starting with the pot that cooks the mash at 175 degrees and ending with the moonshine in the proofing barrel. This is a highly technical process that takes years to learn and perfect. But after this the episode simplifies moonshine brewing through Popcorn footage. The super 8 footage has a poor visual quality compared to the digital material in the episode. Popcorn's legitimacy appears less through the details he offers on how he brews and more through the legends he tells of his brew. He claims a pint he is brewing will cause four fights and another pint he brewed caused a married couple to divorce. Some batches he made were for happiness, and others led to sadness. Here the archival footage establishes that there is artistry to making moonshine. It is not a technical skill per se but a form of expression that shapes the emotional complexities of a community. Most importantly, the footage conveys a primitive community where happiness is established through basic arts such as moonshining.

The serial narrative of *Moonshiners*' first season shows the timeless struggles of moonshiners to evade law enforcement. The plot of Tim and Tickle differs in some ways from Popcorn's. Tim and Tickle successfully evade the task force that appears to be on their trail throughout the season. Meanwhile, the police finally raid Popcorn's farm in Parrotsville, Tennessee, in 2009 and are perched to bring the legendary moonshiner to jail. But both plots

stress how the love of making moonshine outweighs any possible consequences from United States institutions. During a brew in "The Law Comes
Knockin" episode, Tickle talks directly to the camera and states:

> The risks of moonshining are great risks. You know? It's just like any
> other thing that you are gonna do that's, well, not legal. But this is
> what I gotta do to help survive, and I do it because it's something that
> I love. And, I mean, what can you replace something that you love
> with? Nothing.

Throughout the first season, archival footage of Popcorn constantly portrays
the moonshiner's passion for his craft through his lyrical vignettes, but the
last episode moves to a somber tone as Popcorn's wife recounts how he
committed suicide rather than face arrest. The interviews stress how Popcorn
would rather not live than to live life in a correctional facility where he
couldn't partake in his region's artful traditions. Tim, Tickle, and Popcorn
are committed to living life outside of the law within traditions passed down
through generations.

Alaska: The Last Frontier establishes the primitive community of golden
ages by looking at the historical roots of one self-sufficient family, the
Kilchers. The premiere episode constructs life in Alaska as a retreat from
the problems of industrial civilizations, which are shown to be evil at
their core. This happens most explicitly when we hear about patriarch Yule
Kilcher's immigration from Switzerland eighty years ago to escape both
Hitler and a European continent being devoured by war through global
power struggles. Yule assumed Hitler was going to take over the world,
so he looked to Alaska's geographic exclusionism as a way to retreat from
society and live a subsistence lifestyle outside of the capitalist economic
system. In the opening credits, Yule's grandson claims that, to him, Alaska
means, "not having to be supported by the man or the grocery store.
You gotta go out there, and you gotta be aggressive and do whatever it
takes to put food on the table." "The man" mentioned here personifies a
socioeconomic system that the Kilcher family avoids to pursue an ideal
life. The series shows how three generations of Kilchers continue Yule's
homesteading vision of pastoral utopianism. The season boils life down to

three essentials: (1) preparing your house for winter, (2) cutting firewood for winter, and (3) hunting for food for winter. This subsistence living continually offers the Kilchers a rural retreat from society.

Many of these rural shows isolate rural spaces from American society through their fixations with mapping. *Moonshiners*, for example, transitions between scenes by using a topographic map of a region that includes mountain ranges, roads, and towns to show where moonshiners are working. These moments entail the camera slowly panning across a region such as Southeastern Virginia and then zooming in on a smaller section of the place, ultimately to have a thumb tack digitally drop to show where the moonshiners are on the map. *Swamp People* also uses maps to transition between scenes. The map is digitally created and lacks the detailed markers of a topographic map, but it conveys the waters of Southeastern Louisiana. The map transition begins on a very small area with an X and the name of the

Figure 5.1 The simplicity of the rural golden age. Atz Lee Kilcher prepares for winter by cutting firewood on *Alaska: The Last Frontier*.

hunter in the previous scene. The camera then zooms out to a larger view of the region and then an X appears where the next scene will take place. The name of the hunter then appears on the screen as the camera pans and zooms in on that specific locale. The maps create a pastoralism whereby the country is divorced from the city and society in general. The maps present the rural areas as self-contained, first and foremost spatially, but by extension, culturally.

The world constructed on rural reality shows is brutal, but the shows present the country through mythic pastoralism whereby brutality appears through long-established, often ancient themes, not the political economy of expulsions. One of the main themes in *Alaska: The Last Frontier* is humanity versus nature. The show stresses the extreme harshness of the Alaskan winter; if humans do not prepare properly for the winter through stockpiling wood and food, they will die. The ability of one to continue to live in a place over the years is boiled down to a simplistic ability to plan. *Swamp People* investigates the conflicts of humans versus beasts. There are two immediate threats to human life on the show. First, episodes detail the proper procedures for killing an alligator and explain how failures to follow the steps can result in the hunter falling prey to the gators. We learn how to pull in lines with caught gators to bring them to the surface without falling in the water. We learn the proper way to shoot an alligator. Failure to hit a gator in a quarter-sized kill spot on the back of the head will result in the alligator surviving and potentially killing the hunter. Other episodes tell the story of an alligator coming close to a human swimming spot. These episodes follow a specific hunter tracking down the threatening alligator so that humans remain unharmed. *Moonshiners* explores the conflicts between outlaws and civilization. The moonshiner is always portrayed as a moral person who makes liquor to follow his passion and to bring joy to the community. But like a western, the series focuses on law enforcement in a way that threatens to capture the outlaw. The unjust law enforcer always threatens to imprison the just moonshiner.

The nostalgia on these programs is predicated on white heterosexual masculinity. Tim and Tickle are white men with wives and children, just like Popcorn Sutton was. Despite Yule Kilcher having six daughters, *Alaska: The Last Frontier* focuses on the lives of Yule's two sons, Otto and Atz, and their children and grandchildren. The wives on this program are shown in domestic roles, as they stay inside and prepare food while their husbands chop firewood and hunt. Often *Swamp People* follows white father-and-son teams such as Troy and Jacob Landry, Mike and T-Mike Kliebert, Bruce and Junior Mitchell, and Joe LaFont and his stepson Tommy Chauvin. Season Three follows two brothers, Glenn and Mitchell Guist, who spent their lives on the swamp. The ability to escape the political economy of expulsions is predicated on escaping from feminist, anti-racist, and LGBTQ concerns.

When the shows stray from this privileged, white male, heterosexual identity, they do so by explaining how the exceptionalism of the alternative identities is couched in historical traditions. Tenth-generation African American alligator hunter Albert "Butch" Knight is introduced in the "Force of Nature" episode of *Swamp People*'s first season. Immediately the episode includes a vignette with archival photographs to explain the origins of African Americans in Louisiana and why some became alligator hunters. The narrator states: "African Americans' roots in Louisiana date back to 1717 when the French brought the first slaves to work the plantations. Escaped slaves often fled to the swamp, the place where they could more easily avoid recapture."

The images move from slaves working in the field for a master to two African Americans pulling a killed alligator out of the swamp with the help of two horses. Through this vignette, the very presence of a black alligator hunter in the swamp has a premodern feel to it. However, Season One also makes Butch's knowledge passed down from generation to generation less applicable to the swamp than the knowledge passed down by whites. Butch's family hunts by staking wooden posts in the middle of the swamp with hooked lines tied to them, a strategy that allows them to capture the biggest alligators who don't travel near the shoreline where all the white hunters hunt. But the season shows how Butch and his sons routinely fall way short of his goal to capture gators for his sixty tags. Moreover, Butch's historical relationship to the land is jeopardized in ways that the white hunters are not. While white sons are fully assimilated into a historical tradition of passing down hunting identities, Butch's black sons have moved to New Orleans and only come to the swamp to help their dad meet his tags. While the white sons sincerely learn the traits of their parents, Butch's sons fall in the water at points and seem inept, a clear sign that the African American swamper's legacy is threatened. African Americans are othered on the show by losing their historical continuity to the land.

Native American alligator hunters on the show are celebrated and othered because their indigenous status grants them a longer and more authentic connection to the swamp. The "Hunters or Hunted?" episode of Season Two introduces R.J. and his son Jay Paul, members of the Native American Houma tribe. R.J.'s first line is "The swamp belongs to the Native Americans, because we were here first." The narrator explains that the Houmas settled in Louisiana before 1682, 100 years before the Cajuns, as archival drawings of Houmas steering boats through the swamps appear on screen. This longer history gives R.J. and Jay Paul a bond with the land that is more natural. The episode includes confessionals and plots that draw on the noble savage stereotype that positions Native Americans as having a mystical relationship to the land. Jay Paul says, "Wildlife is our culture. We listen to mother nature, so mother nature is everything to us." The episode shows R.J. and Jay Paul using hunting techniques that are supposedly not known to white hunters. These techniques are presented as magical. The narrator says R.J. has a special ritual, and then R.J. says, "We're gonna do a magic touch on this one. We're gonna bless this one." The narrator then says R.J. is spreading "an ancient potent mixture of blood and chicken juice." Here the othering is a celebration of a stronger connection that Native Americans have to the swamp than whites do.

Interestingly, female alligator hunters lack any historical relationship to place other than turning to this profession to reconnect with their family's patriarch. Liz Cavalier makes her first appearance in Season Two simply as Troy's occasional assistant, but Season Three follows her as she hunts in a female team with Kristi Broussard. Liz explains how alligator hunting allows her to remember life with her father, who recently passed away. Teary eyed, Liz explains how she often uses his old hooks, which are not as effective as newer ones, but which hold sentimental and spiritual value to her. There is no archival footage of when women started to hunt alligators. Rather, the episode includes grainy VHS footage of Liz's father hunting as she recounts how she grew up the daughter of a champion alligator hunter. Kristi's story is also tied to her patriarchal line, as she says she grew up hunting with her dad, brothers, and male cousins. Her status as a hunter is an anomaly created through her tomboy status. The women on the show are more problematic in terms of the nostalgia they invoke, so they don't have the same connections to land that African American and Native American men do.

Buying Alaska injects rural reality television's fixation on golden ages into the standard reality real estate show so that purchasing a home becomes a way to access utopia. Because the show typically follows first-time home buyers, it does not use the notion of historical roots and a long-standing connection to place that the other rural reality shows do. But the program, more forcefully than the others, stresses that the Alaskan country offers an escape from contemporary cities. The narration in the opening credits powerfully introduce this theme. A narrator says,

> This is Alaska—
> The last American Frontier.
> These are the dreamers
> Who want to leave the manic rush of the city behind
> And own a piece of the untamed North.
> From boathouses to outhouses,
> From the bare essentials to just plain bears,
> This is the last American outpost of wilderness.
> For these adventurous homebuyers, it's Alaska or bust.

The opening credits create a different type of nostalgia, one for nineteenth- and early twentieth-century westward travel when the American West was still undeveloped and offered an alternative unsettled lifestyle to eastern urbanism. Alaska is positioned as a space that resurrects older tropes of American identity.

The show continually emphasizes details that set the properties apart from typical city and even rural life in the United States in order to convey rural utopia through older ways of living. Buyers frequently drive to homes with their realtors on off-road vehicles, as the homes are not accessible on paved roads. Outhouses, the lack of running water, and how the homes are not connected to the electric grid become desired selling points. While *Alaska: The Last Frontier* shows the hard, often brutal work required to survive an Alaskan winter off the grid, *Buying Alaska* features joyous home buyers who want to pursue this lifestyle. It is never presented as a hardship. Framing shots of the property before and after the house tour emphasizes the scenic beauty of nature and living in harmony with wildlife. In episodes where couples look at houses on waterfronts, editors splice images of the bay, whales, and seals. Homes set in the woods are usually introduced with montages of nearby mountains, rivers, streams, and bears.

Buying Alaska uses a mapping graphic similar to the one on *Swamp People* in order to convey how removed from civilization the home buyers want to be. Before each home tour, we see a map of Alaska in its entirety where the water is blue and the state is green. The mountain ranges are raised, and the city of Anchorage is the only named location. The camera quickly zooms to the area where the couple is looking for a home. If a town is nearby, it will be shown by a yellow dot, and the property is shown with a red arrow. Season Three, Episode Four, for example, has a couple looking at homes not connected to roads that are fifteen miles away from Talkeetna, whose population is less than 1,000. The maps show markers of traditional living, whether a larger city or small town, to show how far the buyers would go to escape that lifestyle.

All of these shows are united in the way that sincerity constructs rural communities as primitive. Whereas urban reality shows such as *Vanderpump Rules* (2013–present) and *The Real Housewives* (2006–present) focus on melodramatic fighting between contestants, rural reality shows emphasize the teamwork and cooperation required to live outside a modern, industrialized capitalist economy. *Swamp People* focuses on how an alligator hunting duo work together. If one cast member is not upholding his responsibilities as part of the team, those professional failures do not lead to any fights. Rather, they offer the opportunity for shameful reflection to help to inspire the troubled worker to try harder. This occurs with Mike Kliebert's son T-Mike, who frequently falls off the boat because he is not concentrating when he is setting lines or pulling in alligators for his father to shoot. At a family dinner in Season One, T-Mike reflects on how he is failing to live up to family traditions and vows to work harder. The focus on the wellbeing of everyone in the primitive communities redeems the problemed son on *Alaska: The Last Frontier*, as well. Atz Lee is portrayed as the prodigal Kilcher who left the family homestead for rebellious years in other towns and then returned to work hard as a family member. While all of the other Kilchers hunt, harvest food, and secure firewood for the winter, Atz Lee procrastinates and doesn't go hunting until the first snowfall nears. Atz Lee fails to prepare for the winter, but his family comes together to help him and his wife survive the brutal cold on the homestead.

As Williams argues, golden ages speak to the way our desire for stability glosses over pressing social and spatial problems, and we can see two distinct sets of problems hidden throughout these rural reality programs. First, these programs offer a release from urban problems in the political economy of expulsions by simplistically looking to the country as the city's foil. These shows suggest that a person can still live in one place throughout his or her life and that a person can achieve oneness with a locale. In this sense, the country remains out of reach from the political economy of social expulsions grasping America's global cities. These programs set up a structure where we can fix urban problems of American global cities merely by longing for the country. But on another level, the country comes to stand for a relationship with a space that was also achievable in industrial cities. From the 1870s through the 1970s, Americans could live for generations in cities. They set up roots in ethnic and racial neighborhoods. Rural reality shows offer a multigenerational approach to living in a space that Americans used to have in city spaces.

Second, the rural tranquility on these programs offers a retreat from the problems threatening to expel people from these areas. Saskia Sassen reminds us that rural areas are open to predatory lending, rising costs of living, loss of industry, and environmental problems. This aspect of rural life is completely ignored on rural reality television shows with golden ages. For example, the Gulf oil spill, considered the worst oil spill in United States history, occurred on April 20, 2010 when an explosion led to a BP pipe leaking continuous oil into the waters off Louisiana. The pipe was not capped until July 15, resulting in an estimated 3.19 million barrels of oil spilling into the Gulf Coast ecosystem. This not only devastated wildlife; it also devastated fishermen and women who earn their living from working the waters off Louisiana. Documentarian Josh Fox opens *Gasland II* (2013) with a segment on the Gulf oil spill. Chemist and MacArthur

Recipient Wilma Subra explains the spill has resulted in the loss of the Gulf as a productive ecosystem but not as a productive source of fossil fuel. Fox then has Kindra Arnesen, a fisherman's wife, explain the impact of the devastation. She argues this isn't about losing an income. It's about the loss of a way of life—the ability to go on the bayou with your family, catch food, and commune with nature. Arnesen says, "We are gonna have a dead fishery, contaminated land, a bag full of bills, and a court date when the federal government tells BP that their cleanup has been completed. Why stay?" Fox then offers a voice-over narration that puts the spill most explicitly in terms of what Sassen sees as expulsions. He says, "That's when it hit me. How much of this whole culture was gonna have to move?" Five weeks after the oil spill in the Gulf was capped, *Swamp People* premiered. The Atchafalaya River Basin where *Swamp People* films was not only affected by the 2010 Gulf spill; it has also been affected by eleven spills from smaller companies since 2002.[4] None of this is mentioned on *Swamp People*, where the waters of rural Louisiana offer access to lands untainted by social progress. There is also a complete evasion of environmental hazards and expulsions in the Alaskan reality shows. Homes for sale on bays offer access to a primitive relationship with nature on *Buying Alaska*. The program never brings up rising sea levels due to global warming and how bayside homes might go underwater in upcoming years. The seas are meant to be fished. The firewood is meant to be burned. There are no mentions of PCB contamination in the fish or the way that towns such as Fairbanks where wood burning stoves are the main source of heating cause the air quality level to be worse than the city of Beijing.[5]

FOOL'S GOLD: *HERE COMES HONEY BOO BOO* AND THE AFFIRMATION OF THE URBAN

Another way that rural reality programs support the political economy of urban expulsions is through deriding the country. These shows make the country seem so backward that viewers aspire to the opposite values to those seen on the screen. Compared to the deranged spectacles in these shows, urban life and urban reality television seem like needed anchors of civilization. TLC's *Here Comes Honey Boo Boo* works in this way. The show premiered on August 8, 2012 and was a spin-off of TLC's *Toddlers and Tiaras* (2009–present), which focused on the lives of young pageant contestants and their parents, often of the lower socio-economic class. *Here Comes Honey Boo Boo* is set in McIntyre, Georgia, population 650. It follows the family life of one of *Toddlers and Tiaras* most unforgettable cast members, Alana "Honey Boo Boo" Thompson, a sassy six-year-old whose exuberant approach to life is expressed through flailing arms, fast talk, and a thick rural southern accent that often needs subtitles. The program's real star became Alana's mom, "Mama June" Shannon. She served as a narrator of sorts for the show, explaining through confessionals what the family was doing and why. Often she would translate poor rural culture for viewers not in this demographic, noting, for example, that the Redneck Games were like the Olympics, only with missing teeth and exposed butt cracks. Other members of the show include Alana's father, Sugar Bear, and June's daughters to different men: Jessica, whose nickname is Chubs; Anna, whose nickname is Chickadee; and Lauryn, whose nickname is Pumpkin.

As a TLC show, *Here Comes Honey Boo Boo* was part of what critics such as Michael Starr call TLC's "freak show" brand.[6] TLC focused on programs where the family was defined as abnormal; that is, the family fell outside of the middle-class suburban ideal of a mother, father, and two or three children, all of whom are able bodied. *Jon and Kate Plus 8* (2007–09) features a Pennsylvania couple with a set of twins and sextuplets. *The Little Couple* (2009–present) follows a family of dwarfs. *19 Kids and Counting* (2009–15) chronicles the lives of the Duggar family, who have more than nineteen children. The channel also features shows such as *My 600 Pound Life* (2012–present), which follows morbidly obese people. Although Kevin Glynn and Joshua Gamson have theorized television shows about people labeled as freaks as carnival-esque spaces where the abnormal claims a right to speak, Jennifer Maher and Kirsten Pike have not found such a liberating structure of freakiness on TLC.[7] Pike, in fact, argues spectacles of abnormality on TLC reinforce cultural norms. It is within this trajectory that the spatial politics of *Here Comes Honey Boo Boo* emerge. The country is presented as freakishly backward through a lens that privileges contemporary urban sensibilities.

The second episode of Season One, "Gonna Be a Glitz Pig," incorporates this place-based viewing structure into the plot. Mama June hires

Barbara Hickey of The Etiquette School of Atlanta to come to her house and teach Alana and Pumpkin to be refined. Hickey approaches the house with a noticeable undercurrent of disgust, although she pretends to treat June, Alana, and Pumpkin with respect. June holds the family's pet pig in her arms. Immediately the episode presents us with a scene that violates urban sensibilities, as pigs are seen as farm animals, not indoor pets. Barbara Hickey's first statement in the scene is "This is one of those pet pigs," an innocent statement, but the mild-level of horror on her face shows how these country practices are repulsive to an urbanite. The sound editing heightens the violation of norms, as the pig's squeals drown out the conversation between Hickey and the family. The irony of the introduction comes when Hickey tells Alana that it is proper to shake someone's hand when you meet them. As Alana walks down the porch steps to shake Hickey's hand, the pig's grunts register at an uncomfortable audio level, making the family the exact opposite of those with manners. As Hickey lectures the girls on etiquette in the home, Alana frantically clenches her hands, moves her arms, and rubs her belly. Pumpkin sits slouched over with her legs up on the couch. Hickey's patience is tested with the uncultured country girls. When Pumpkin says, "I don't care what people think of me. I am who I am. If you don't like me, you don't like me," Hickey says in frustration, "Aaaaaand, I hope that works for you." The second part of the lesson is on table manners. As Hickey lectures the girls on how to take the napkin from the table and place it on their laps, Pumpkin uses the napkin to blow her nose. Then Pumpkin asks Hickey, "Can you fart at the table?" Hickey responds, "That is probably the height of rudeness." Then the scene cuts to an interview with Hickey who says, "There are some habits we have to break. The bodily function—we don't do that," as she smiles smugly, completely reassured that her urban way is correct and Alana's family's is not.

The first season takes a condescending view of rural life in McIntyre through the way it equates the country with human waste, disease, and bad health. The season fixates on bowel movements and flatulence. In Episode One, Mama June and her daughters decide they need to lose weight, and the girls sincerely recount Mama June's weight-loss secret of passing gas twelve to fifteen times a day. The opening credits of Season One and Two show the family posing for a picture when one of them passes gas loudly.

Figure 5.2 Alana's pet pig helps to show how backward the country is on *Here Comes Honey Boo Boo.*

TLC/Photofest ©TLC

Many scenes are shot in the family's dining room, and the most noticeable items in the room are the plastic shelves filled with hundreds of rolls of toilet paper. This becomes a topic of conversation in Episode Three, "She Ooooo'd Herself," when the girls and Mama June discuss how everyone in the world could go to the bathroom in their house and there would still be leftover toilet paper. The hoarding aesthetic of the house is framed as a disease in Episode Three when Mama June says she is addicted to extreme couponing and buying in bulk. The country as a place of disease also appears in Episode One, "This is My Crazy Family," when the family attends the Redneck Games. First, Pumpkin enters the "Bobbing for Pig's Feet" competition, and Mama June wonders how much bacteria the raw animal parts could have, even though she allows her daughter to compete. Then the family walks to a lake on the premises and reads a warning sign that there is flesh eating bacteria in the water and that no one should swim. The scene then edits in people swimming in the water to the sound of banjo music. Other episodes fixate on how country life offers poor physical health. Although Mama June realizes she and her family members are obese and need to lose weight, she attends auctions and buys cartons of cupcakes and bags of junk food. Season Two includes two episodes in which Sugar Bear is hospitalized for pneumonia and pancreatitis.

The country also stands out as a place of flawed work ethics and misguided financial management strategies. In "This is My Crazy Family" Mama June explains to viewers that Sugar Bear works seven days a week; she goes on to say that she and her children do not work but sleep until one or two in the afternoon. Mama June and Sugar Bear lack the discipline and drive to be a couple able to earn and save money through middle-class and upper-class jobs with 9 a.m. to 5 p.m. work days and weekends off. Moreover, the show fixates on how expensive it is for Mama June to pay for Alana's pageants. Pike astutely notes that pageant life on *Toddlers and Tiaras* presents the moms as bad financial managers in need of control from their skeptical husbands, but the out-of-control nature of Mama June's financial planning takes on a different life on *Here Comes Honey Boo Boo*, where episodes focus on how Mama June can save money in some areas to spend it on Alana's pageants. But Mama June lacks the discipline to save her money wisely. When she goes to an auction looking to buy clothes for her eldest daughter's soon-to-be-born baby, she winds up buying only cakes and potato chips.

As *Here Comes Honey Boo Boo* evolved, it showed Mama June and her family in more sincere ways, but it found new ways to showcase cast members as lacking proper manners. In fact, the program often highlighted a repulsive, crude gesture after a heartwarming sincere moment to remind viewers that Mama June and her family should be laughed at. Season Two plots Sugar Bear's decision to propose to Mama June, offering up a traditional love story that appeals to viewers of all classes. Episode Four, "Hubba Bubba," has Sugar Bear talking with Alana and June's other children about his desire to marry June and become Pumpkin, Chubs, and Chickadee's stepfather. Although Sugar Bear proposes to June in the dining room, with June sitting in front of all the toilet paper, he speaks about love in terms of emotions, commitment, and partnership in ways that many can relate to. Reluctant to enter any marriage, June agrees to a commitment ceremony to show her love for Sugar Bear. After a sweet scene, Pumpkin says she has to "take a piss," a crudeness which punctuates the scene with laughter and reminds the viewers that their identification with June and her family is limited. Likewise, Season Four ends with June's oldest daughter, Anna, moving out of June's house to Alabama. The family is heartbroken, since Anna's daughter, Kaitlyn, will also leave the family home. In a confessional, Pumpkin notes that she will miss Kaitlyn because she is "immune to her." The director then mocks her by pointing out what most people immediately realize: Pumpkin does not know the meaning of the word immune. He asks her, "Do you even know what immune means?" The scene delivers ironic humor when she explains that immunity means you are used to something, so she is immune to Kaitlyn because she is used to having her around. The difference between our understanding of immunity and Pumpkin's is the difference, according to the show, between proper urban perspectives and backward country ones.

But even as the series started to inject more sincerity into country life, it also included plots and scenes that were there just to disgust viewers with country practices that violate our basic understanding of civilization. For example, the first episode of Season Two, "The Manper," includes Mama June and her family finding roadkill. They take the carcass of a crushed hog home to skin it and eat the meat. June frames this act as a good way to save money, but most viewers read the scene as a violation of the proper agricultural procedures that insure that an animal is killed and preserved in a hygienic way. This scene violates the viewer's basic understanding of what it means to be a person. It mediates a place where one would never want to live. Urbanity is the better option.

The fact that TLC chose to cancel Here Comes Honey Boo Boo in October 2014 because Mama June was secretly dating a convicted child molester is the ultimate demonstration of the country's repulsive backwardness. The fifth season was already shot and edited when TMZ broke the story that Mama June was dating Mark McDaniel, who was released from jail after serving ten years for molestation. The story became seedier when June's eldest daughter Anna appeared on HLN's Dr. Drew on Call (2010–16) two weeks later and announced that McDaniel molested her when she was in the third grade. June's response at the time, Anna said, was angry and dismissive. Furthermore, Anna says June turned Pumpkin against her by claiming

McDaniel is Pumpkin's father. These tragic events add sexual abuse, perversion, and broken family life onto a long list of abnormality associated with country life that one should reject by embracing more urban values.

CONCLUSION

And so this book comes to an end with another example of how reality television negotiates place-based identities to win our consent for the spatial politics of expulsions. When something such as the political economy of social expulsions occurs, it requires cultural artifacts that help to justify it to people and win their consent. Since 1980, cities have transformed from industrial centers that housed all classes to fuel manufacturing to financial centers in a global economy that have room for only the extremely rich and the abject poor. Many people have been forced to leave cities where their families have lived for generations because the areas are no longer affordable. Based strictly on the social and economic aspects of this transformation in urban life, many would reject cities as spaces of brutality that can only house the privileged and the destitute. Reality television is one site able to convince us of accepting this new configuration of classed urban space by the way it places residual urbanisms in the new city to make it seem like today's cities still serve the interests of all classes.

Part of this process of winning consent comes through the visual aesthetics of reality television, which beautify the sanitized closed spaces of contemporary urban life. While contemporary cities appear on screen, older urbanisms appear through plots, sounds, and identities that were part of previous ways of urban living in America. These bits and pieces of the past make it seem like the contemporary city is still home to a variety of socioeconomic groups who have been expelled from America's global cities. Reality television casts older people who retained New York accents that filled the city during the industrial era. Reality television includes plots of entrepreneurs moving up in social class and pursuing the American dream in cities where this was achievable during the industrial era. Reality television transforms global cities into gaming spaces where contestants of all classes could compete. Reality television makes stars out of people who embody residual class-based racial or ethnic identities of specific cities. Travelling back in time on rural reality shows upholds contemporary urban sensibilities either by naïvely recalling a pastoral golden age that offers a brief escape from the city or by rejecting older ways of country life as uncivilized and revolting.

When urban reality shows lack nostalgia, they win our consent for the political economy of social expulsions by othering service industry workers. The servants' and servers' backward behavior or status as somehow less than human makes the elite redeemable figures, even though they come to stand for the closed spatial politics of cities. The elite appear to us as normal because the servants and servers appear so abnormal, and this normalization of the rich justifies the political economy of social expulsions that enables their wealth.

This book attempts to raise critical media literacy about place-based identities on reality television in hopes of encouraging equality-minded social justice. While these politically committed literacies will not stop the political economy of expulsions, they are an important first step in rejecting the nostalgic celebration of urban life on reality television. Populations are being evicted from cities and rural areas. Instead of celebrating them as central to spaces on reality television, we should remember the pains of their loss of home, the sadness of their loss of culture, and the brutality they experience in the current economy.

We should also remember that the future generation of storytellers on reality television are sitting in our classrooms right now. The way that America's global cities have closed off residency to the elite and the poor does not have to result in a shutting down of spatial relationships in society or on reality television. The way that America's global cities have restricted residency to the elite and the poor does not have to result in reality television trying to win our consent for the political economy of social expulsions. We can look to the history of the genre to see that it once welcomed an open construction of space. Recall that the historical argument of the book is that reality television went from offering an open construction of urban spatial relations in the twentieth century to winning our consent of closed spatial relationships in the twenty-first century. In the twentieth century, reality television went into spaces open to all classes and found ways to open up oppressive spatial relationships for just purposes. *Candid Camera* (1948–67, first run) challenged the spatial isolation of women in the suburbs. *An American Family* (1973) challenged the way manifest destiny set up the West as an idealized space for the patriarchal nuclear family. *The Real World* (1992–present) refused to allow its characters to stay within the gentrified neighborhood of SoHo and instead used the area as a transportation hub to urban areas written out of the gentrified imagination. How can the future storytellers of reality television re-inject the genre with an open construction of space so that we see the dignity of servants and servers, so that we allow servers to challenge their oppression, so that we visualize and narrate the stories of the people expelled from cities, and so that we call attention to and challenge the expulsions of rural areas? How would this require a rejection of the genre's focus on time-shifting and othering? Could nostalgia be used to open contemporary spatial politics rather than merely asking us to accept dominant ones? This is the lesson I hope the book imparts to future reality television storytellers—that the current trends in reality television's spatial politics are just that, trends. We can rework space.

NOTES

1 Raymond Williams, *The Country and the City* (New York: Oxford University Press, 1973), 17.

2 Raymond Williams, *The Country and the City* (New York: Oxford University Press, 1973), 1.

3 Raymond Williams, *The Country and the City* (New York: Oxford University Press, 1973), 35–45.

4 Ken Wells, Aaron Kurlioff, and Charles R. Babvock, "Oil Spills in Most Imperiled U.S. Coastal Wetland Escapes Fines," *Bloomberg Business Review*, February 3, 2011. Accessed May 30, 2016. http://www.bloomberg.com/news/articles/2011-02-03/oil-spills-in-most-imperiled-u-s-coastal-wetland-escape-fines.

5 Kim Murphy, "Fairbanks Area, Trying to Stay Warm, Chokes on Wood Stove Pollution," *Los Angeles Times*, February 13, 2013. Accessed May 30, 2016. http://articles.latimes.com/2013/feb/16/nation/la-na-fairbanks-air-pollution-20130217.

6 Michael Starr, "Toddlers & Trash: TLC Has Built a Network on Exploitation—Is It Any Wonder Why It's Blowing Up in Their Face?" *New York Post*, May 24, 2015, 15.

7   Kevin Glynn, *Tabloid Culture: Trash Taste, Popular Power, and the Transformation of American Television* (Durham, NC: Duke University Press, 2000); Joshua Gamson, *Freaks Talk Back: Tabloid Talk Shows and Sexual Nonconformity* (Chicago, IL: University of Chicago Press, 1999); Jennifer Maher, "What Do Women Watch? Tuning In To the Compulsory Heterosexuality Channel," in Susan Murray and Laurie Ouellette, eds, *Realty TV: Remaking Television Culture*, 1st edition (New York: New York University Press, 2004), 197–213; Kirsten Pike, "Freaky Five-Year-Olds and Mental Mommies: Narratives of Gender, Race, and Class in TLC's *Toddlers & Tiaras*," in Brenda Weber, ed., *Reality Gendervision: Sexuality & Gender on Transatlantic Reality Television* (Durham, NC: Duke University Press, 2014), 282–98.

QUESTIONS FOR DISCUSSION

These discussion questions are designed to help students locate the key arguments and terms of chapters. They are designed to help undergraduate students fully comprehend the chapters.

INTRODUCTION

1. Turn to the opening section of the introduction.

    a. Why is it important to study portraits of city space on reality television?
    b. What is the main contradiction between American global cities in real life and American global cities on reality television?
    c. What does the term *the political economy of social expulsions* mean?
    d. What does the term *space* mean?
    e. What is cognitive mapping, and how do reality television programs help us cognitively map city space?
    f. What is hegemony, and why is this an important term for studying the way reality television presents space?
    g. What is the main argument of the book?

2. Turn to the section "Open and Closed Spaces in Theory, in Urban Economies, and on Reality Television."

a. What are the two layers of open space? How is the first layer indebted to theorist Doreen Massey, and how is the second layer based on urban demography of the industrial era, especially the post-World War II era?

b. How do twentieth-century reality television programs offer open spatial relationships?

c. What does the term *closed spaces* mean in this book? How are closed urban spaces a result of key transformations in the economy that began in the 1980s? What are those transformations?

d. How do Chapters Two through Five show reality television helping to win consent for the political economy of social expulsions?

3. Turn to the section "The Definition of Reality Television."

a. How does this book define reality television?

b. Why is Keith Jenkins' view of history brought in to explain the reality television shows selected to study for this book?

c. How can shows such as *Candid Camera, An American Family*, and early seasons of *The Real World* be seen as reality television when they weren't originally classified as reality television?

4. Turn to the section "The Focus on American Reality Television."

a. Why do scholars study the global circulation of reality television?

b. Despite the global reach of reality television, what is the value of studying American reality television's portraits of American global cities?

5. Turn to the section "What We Can Accomplish by Telling the History of Reality Television from the Perspective of Urban Space."

a. Why is developing a critical media literacy about the political economy of social expulsions an important step toward creating equality minded social change?

b. How is developing this critical media literacy about the political economy of social expulsions relevant to Doreen Massey's point that spatial relationships are never set?

CHAPTER ONE

1. Turn to the opening section in this chapter. The chapter explores twentieth-century reality television's macro-level engagement with open space, but it also insists there are micro-level differences between the ways *Candid Camera*, *An American Family*, and *The Real World* engage open urban space. What are those micro-level differences?

2. Turn to the section "Turning Ordinary Places into Extraordinary Spaces on *Candid Camera*."

    a. How is space on *Candid Camera* simultaneously specific and generic, and how does this relate to the show's dual format?

    b. How does the generic depiction of space on *Candid Camera* resonate with the class structures of post-World War II industrial cities?

    c. How does the generic depiction of space on *Candid Camera* resonate with the way that post-World War II network television re-organized spatial relationships?

    d. How did Allen Funt's contradictory relationship to class structures shape his generic construction of space on *Candid Camera*?

    e. How did Funt's figure of the provocateur and his theory of "the average man in a small crisis" open space on *Candid Camera*?

    f. How did *Candid Camera* open space for women in post-World War II America?

3. Turn to the section "Opening Space Through Power Geometries in *An American Family*."

    a. What are power geometries, according to Doreen Massey, and how do they shape the politics of travel in *An American Family*?

    b. What are the aesthetic trends and technological devices of the Direct Cinema movement, and how does *An American Family* producer Craig Gilbert use them?

    c. How does Episode One of *An American Family* represent the concept of manifest destiny and family life in the space of Santa Barbara?

    d. How does *An American Family*, from the second episode on, use power geometries to open the spatial relationships of family life in Santa Barbara?

e. How did *An American Family* resonate with post-World War II economic egalitarianism by being part of PBS' educational mission?

4. Turn to the section "The Gentrified Neighborhood as Transportation Hub: Open Space on MTV's *The Real World*, Season One."

   a. How are gentrified neighborhoods such as SoHo closed spaces, and how did Season One of *The Real World* use the geographic construct of the transportation hub to open space in New York City?

   b. How did this open construction of space on Season One of *The Real World* fit with MTV's branding goals in the early 1990s?

   c. What are some examples of the loft serving as a transportation hub to open space to other parts of the city on this season of *The Real World*?

   d. How did *The Real World* construct space by employing MTV's postmodern aesthetic?

5. Turn to the conclusion.

   a. How did the show COPS show the closing of space on reality television during the early stages of the political economy of social expulsions?

   b. Why did reality television need to change from advocating the closed nature of space on COPS to winning the consent of the closed nature of space on twenty-first-century reality television programs?

CHAPTER TWO

1. Turn to the opening section in this chapter.

   a. Why is diasporic nostalgia a useful theoretical construct to think about the way that Americans view city spaces on twenty-first-century reality television?

   b. How does the reflective nature of diasporic nostalgia play out along the visuals, sounds, and premises of the city on contemporary reality television shows?

c. How do the visuals, sounds, and premises of twenty-first-century urban reality television shows work together to win our consent for the political economy of social expulsions?

2. Turn to the section "The Specticality of the Closed City on Reality Television."

a. Why is spectacle a useful term to think about the visual presentation of the city on twenty-first-century reality television?
b. Where do spectacles of the city occur within episodes?
c. How do the spectacles of the city work to present the city as a sanitized area for the elite?

3. Turn to the section "Social Intimacy and Nostalgia for Postwar Class Equality: The Sounds of the City and Show Premises."

a. Svetlana Boym argues that social intimacy is a crucial aspect of diasporic nostalgia. What does she mean by social intimacy, and why is it a useful way to think about the nostalgia we feel when we watch twenty-first-century reality television programs about the city?
b. How do local accents on urban reality television shows register older urban identities and create a social intimacy that is part of diasporic nostalgia?
c. How does the premise of the family business on many urban reality shows register older urban identities, and what types of intimacies are created on reality programs about family businesses?
d. CBS's The Amazing Race uses the concept of the level playing field in its competition. What is the level playing field, how does it work on The Amazing Race, and how does it create a social intimacy based on diasporic nostalgia?
e. The premise of the entrepreneur in the city also creates social intimacies that were part of older times in urban cultures. Explain how writings on entrepreneurship during the industrial era envisioned this figure through the American dream and pitted the figure against the capitalist. How do entrepreneurs on contemporary reality programs help us envision older ideas of class and class mobility in contemporary cities?

CHAPTER THREE

1. Turn to the opening section in this chapter.

    a. Why does Bravo invest so much time in bringing urban servants and servers to the screen on the channel's reality programs?
    b. What is meant by the concept of the other? How and why are servants and servers othered on Bravo reality programming?
    c. How do Bravo reality television programs win our consent for the political economy of social expulsions by othering servants and servers?

2. Turn to the section "Contradictory Ideas of Wealth in Bravo's Brand."

    a. What are the branding initiatives at Bravo that made wealthy people on reality shows admirable, and what are the branding initiatives at Bravo that made wealthy people on reality shows hypocritical?
    b. How are Bravo reality programs able to redeem wealthy characters, even though they are mocked?

3. Turn to the section "The Degenerate Server: *Vanderpump Rules*, Orientalism, and the Normalization of the Rich through Geography."

    a. What is Edward Said's theory of orientalism?
    b. How is orientalism a useful construct to think about the relationship between Lisa Vanderpump and her servers on *Vanderpump Rules*?
    c. How are Sur and Lisa's home spaces of normalization on *Vanderpump Rules*?
    d. How does Lisa serve as a psychologist, medical doctor, police officer, and career counselor on the show, and how does this allow her to other and control her servers?
    e. How are servers at risk of becoming uncivilized in spaces outside of Sur and Lisa's home?
    f. How does the whiteness of the servers at Sur give them special privileges that other non-white servers on Bravo do not have? How does the show still position the servers on *Vanderpump Rules* as failures?

4. Turn to the section "The Silent Servant: The Noble Savage in the City on *The Real Housewives*."

   a. What is a noble savage, and how can that figure be translated into urban reality shows in America? How are non-white servants on Bravo sometimes constructed as noble savages? How does the figure of the noble savage other servants?

   b. What are the two main ways that Bravo shows construct servants as noble savages?

5. Turn to the section "The Silly Servant: Hispanic and Latina Stereotypes as Geographic Containment/Expulsion."

   a. How is Cedric Martinez on *The Real Housewives of Beverly Hills* othered through the Latin lover and the bandito stereotypes, and how does this justify his place as an expelled person in the urban political economy?

   b. How is Zoila on *Flipping Out* othered as a Latina maid, and how does this stereotype reinforce her place in the home?

CHAPTER FOUR

1. Turn to the opening section in this chapter.

   a. Why is it important to study Rob Mariano and Tiffany Pollard together? What is the phenomenon in which they partake?

   b. What does it mean to amplify an identity on reality television?

   c. How did amplifying an identity allow Rob Mariano and Tiffany Pollard to create mutually advantageous relationships with a television station?

   d. How do Rob Mariano and Tiffany Pollard help to win our consent for the political economy of social expulsions by the way that they perform urban ethnic and racial identities? What are the key differences between the way that Mariano's ethic identity is performed to win our consent and the way that Pollard's racial identity is performed to win our consent?

2. Turn to the section "Boston Rob's Gameplay: How Ethnic Urban Nostalgia Became Part of CBS's Quest to Become America's Number One Channel through Quality Programming."

   a. When did Little Italies appear in American cities, and what economic trends, from the post-World War II era through today, dispersed their residents?

   b. How does Rob Mariano's performance of Boston Rob register older ethnic urban identities?

   c. What is the imagination of expulsions? How are Rob's performances of Italian American ethnicity on *Survivor* part of the imagination of expulsions?

   d. What is a third space, and what does it mean that Rob's performance of Italian American ethnicity takes place in a third space?

   e. What is the stereotype of the Italian American gangster, and how does Rob's performance of it form the basis of his game play on Seasons Four, Twenty, and Twenty-two of *Survivor*?

   f. What is the stereotype of the Italian American trickster, and how does Rob's performance of it form the basis of his game play on Season Eight of *Survivor* and Season Seven of *The Amazing Race*?

   g. Why was Rob's performance of Italian American identity of interest to CBS executives and the way they envisioned the CBS brand? How did reality television fit into the brand? How did Rob's performance of identity help the channel achieve its goals for reality television?

3. Turn to the section "New York as Sapphire: The Persistence of the Black Ghetto in Contemporary Cities and Its Place in VH1's Evolving Brand."

   a. What place do black poor neighborhoods have in contemporary cities? How is this different from the construction of Little Italies in contemporary cities?

   b. What is the stereotype of the black sapphire, and how does Tiffany Pollard perform it by marrying it to an urban ghetto identity?

    c.   How does Pollard perform the urban sapphire on *I Love New York*, and does it form the basis of her gaming strategy?

    d.   How do New York and Flavor Flav present New York City identity as something larger than life?

    e.   How did Pollard's performance as New York resonate with the branding initiatives at VH1? How did she tie into the channel's focus on irony and camp and also help the channel transition out of its focus on an ironic approach to popular culture nostalgia?

    f.   What does the ironic campiness on programs with New York say about what it takes to win consent of black poverty that is part of the political economy of social expulsions?

CHAPTER FIVE

1.   Turn to the opening section in this chapter.

    a.   Why end this book about urban reality shows with a chapter on rural reality television? According to Raymond Williams, what can stories about the country tell us about the ways we imagine the city?

    b.   What are the two types of rural reality television programs, and how do they help to win consent for the political economy of social expulsions shaping America's global cities?

2.   Turn to the section "Rural Golden Ages."

    a.   Why does Raymond Williams critique the construct of the rural golden age? How can this critique help us think through the way rural reality television programs help to win our consent of the political economy of social expulsions?

    b.   How do rural reality shows use archival footage to help construct a golden age? How does archival footage construct the rural community as primitive?

    c.   How does the fixation on mapping rural space on rural reality shows construct the country community as removed from social progress?

d.   How do rural reality shows depict brutality as a product of nature, not as a product of the political economy of social expulsions?

e.   How do these shows construct a nostalgia for heterosexual white male identities in the country, and how are identities for non-whites and women constructed in relationship to rural space?

f.   What specific environmental aspects of expulsions do rural reality shows ignore to construct the country through pastoral innocence?

3.   Turn to the section "Fool's Gold: *Here Comes Honey Boo Boo* and the Affirmation of the Urban."

a.   How do rural reality shows such as *Here Comes Honey Boo Boo* uphold urban values?

b.   What is TLC's station brand, and how does *Here Comes Honey Boo Boo*'s presentation of country life fit into it?

c.   How is the country presented as a place of derision on Season One of *Here Comes Honey Boo Boo*?

d.   How do other seasons of *Here Comes Honey Boo Boo* present the country more sincerely but still find ways to mock the country?

e.   How do the events that led to the cancelling of *Here Comes Honey Boo Boo* affirm urban values?

REFERENCES

Abu-Lughod, Janet L. *New York, Chicago, Los Angeles: America's Global Cities*. Minneapolis, MN: University of Minnesota Press, 1999.

Altman, Rick. *Film/Genre*. London: British Film Institute, 1999.

Andreeva, Neelie. "Survivor Renewed for Two More Cycles." *Hollywoodreporter.com*, February 26, 2009. Available at: http://www.lexisnexis.com/hottopics/lnacademic#sthash.0UskD1Sg.dpuf. Accessed May 15, 2015.

Andrejevic, Mark. *Reality TV: The Work of Being Watched*. Boulder, CO: Rowman and Littlefield, 2003.

Bale, John. "Virtual Fandoms: Futurescapes of Football." In *Fanatics: Power, Identity, and Fandom in Football*, edited by Adam Brown, 265–78. New York: Routledge, 1998.

Barney, Chuck. "Quality Networks' Theme: Stylized Shows with Intricate Character Development, Sprawling Plots Popular." *Wilkes Barre Times Leader*, August 23, 2006.

Bauman, Zygmunt. *Community: Seeking Safety in an Insecure World*. Malden, MA: Polity, 2001.

Bignell, Jonathan. *Big Brother: Reality TV in the Twenty-First Century*. New York: Palgrave Macmillan, 2005.

Biressi, Anita, and Heather Nunn. *Reality TV: Realism and Revelation*. London: Wallflower Press, 2005.

Boger, John Charles, and Judith Welch Wegener, eds. *Race, Poverty, and American Cities*. Chapel Hill, NC: University of North Carolina Press, 1996.

Bourdieu, Pierre. *Distinctions: A Social Critique of the Judgement of Taste*. Cambridge, MA: Harvard University Press, 1984.

Boym, Svetlana. *The Future of Nostalgia*. New York: Basic Books, 2002.

Butler, Jeremy. *Television Style*, 1st edition. New York: Routledge, 2009.

Caldwell, John Thornton. *Televisuality: Style, Crisis, and Authority in American Television*. New Brunswick, NJ: Rutgers University Press, 1995.

Cavallero, Jonathan. "Gangsters, Fessos, Tricksters, and Sopranos: The Historical Roots of Italian American Stereotype Anxiety." *Journal of Popular Film and Television* 32, no. 3 (June 2004): 50–63.

Chayefsky, Paddy. *Television Plays*. New York: Simon and Schuster, 1955.

Colli, Andrea. *The History of Family Business, 1850–2000*. New York: Cambridge University Press, 2003.

Copple Smith, Erin. "'Affluencers' by Bravo: Defining an Audience Through Cross Promotion." *Popular Communication* 10 (2012): 286–301.

Deery, June. *Consuming Reality: The Commercialization of Factual Entertainment*. New York: Palgrave Macmillan, 2012.

Deery, June. *Reality TV*. London: Polity Press, 2015.

Dovey, Jon. *Freakshow: First Person Media and Factual Television*. London: Pluto Press, 2000.

Dubrofsky, Rachel E. *The Surveillance of Women on Reality Television: Watching the Bachelor and the Bachelorette*. Lanham, MD: Lexington, 2011.

Dwyer, Michael. *Back to the Fifties: Nostalgia, Hollywood Film, and Popular Music of the Seventies and Eighties*. New York: Oxford University Press, 2015.

Dyer, Richard. *White: Essays on Race and Culture*. New York: Routledge, 1997.

Dyer, Richard. *Only Entertainment*, 2nd edition. New York: Routledge, 2002.

Edwards, Leigh H. *The Triumph of Reality TV: The Revolution of American Television*. New York: Praeger, 2012.

Ellingson, T. *The Myth of the Noble Savage*. Berkeley, CA: University of California Press, 2001.

Escoffery, David S., ed. *How Real is Reality TV? Essays on Representation and Truth*. Jefferson, NC: McFarland Press, 2006.

Foucault, Michel. *Discipline and Punish: The Birth of the Prison*. Translated by Alan Sheridan. New York: Vintage, 1979.

Fritch, Robert. *The Assignation of New York*. London: Verso, 1993.

Funt, Allen. *Eavesdroppers at Large: Adventures in Human Nature with Candid Mike and Candid Camera*. New York: Vanguard, 1952.

Funt, Allen with Philip Reed. *Candidly, Allen Funt: A Million Smiles Later*. New York: Barricade, 1994.

Gamson, Joshua. *Freaks Talk Back: Tabloid Talk Shows and Sexual Nonconformity*. Chicago, IL: University of Chicago Press, 1999.

Glynn, Kevin. *Tabloid Culture: Trash Taste, Popular Power, and the Transformation of American Television*. Durham, NC: Duke University Press, 2000.

Goldsmith, William G., and Edward J. Blakely. *Separate Societies: Poverty and Inequality in U.S. Cities*. Philadelphia, PA: Temple University Press, 1992.

Goodwin, Andrew. "Fatal Distractions: MTV Meets Postmodern Theory." In *Sound and Vision: The Music Video Reader*, edited by Simon Frith, Andrew Goodwin, and Lawrence Grossberg, 62–3. New York: Routledge, 1992.

Gray, Herman. *Watching Race: Television and the Struggle for "Blackness."* Minneapolis, MN: University of Minnesota Press, 1995.

Gunning, Thomas. "The Cinema of Attraction[s]: Early Film, Its Spectators and the Avant Garde." In *The Cinema of Attractions Reloaded*, edited by Wanda Strauven, 381–8. Amsterdam: University of Amsterdam Press, 2007.

Harris, Scheena. "Black Women: From Public Arena to Reality TV." In *Real Sister: Stereotypes, Respectability, and Black Women in Reality TV*, edited by Jervette R. Ward, 16–30. New Brunswick, NJ: Rutgers University Press, 2015.

Harvey, David. *Rebel Cities: From the Right to the City to the Urban Revolution*. New York: Verso, 2012.

Hebert, Robert F., and Albert N. Link. *A History of Entrepreneurship*. New York: Routledge, 2009.

Heller, Dana, ed. *Makeover Television: Realities Remodeled*. London: I.B. Taurus, 2007.

Hickey, Magee. "Who Has the Better New York Accent: Sanders or Trump?" Pix11. com, February 10, 2016. Available at: http://pix11.com/2016/02/19/who-has-the-better-new-york-accent-sanders-or-trump/. Accessed July 11, 2016.

Hill, Annette. *Reality TV: Factual Entertainment and Television Audiences*. New York: Routledge, 2005.

Hill, Annette. *Restyling Factual Television: Audiences and News, Documentary, and Reality Genres*. New York: Routledge, 2007.

Homes, Su, and Deborah Jermyn, eds. *Understanding Reality Television*. New York: Routledge, 2004.

Jameson, Frederic. *The Geopolitical Aesthetic: Cinema and Space in the World System*. Bloomington, IN: Indiana University Press, 1992.

Jefferson-James, LaToya. "Selective Reuptake: Perpetuating Misleading Cultural Identity in the Reality Television World." In *Real Sister: Stereotypes, Respectability, and Black Women in Reality TV*, edited by Jervette R. Ward, 31–52. New Brunswick, NJ: Rutgers University Press, 2015.

Jenkins, Henry. *Convergence Culture: Where Old and New Media Collide*. New York: New York University Press, 2007.

Jenkins, Keith. *Re-Thinking History*. New York: Routledge, 1991.

Johnson, Catherine. *Branding Television*. New York: Routledge, 2012.

Kavka, Misha. *Reality Television, Affect, and Intimacy: Reality Matters*. New York: Palgrave Macmillan, 2008.

Kavka, Misha. *Reality TV*. Edinburgh, UK: Edinburgh University Press, 2012.

Kavka, Misha. "Reality TV and the Gendered Politics of Flaunting." In *Reality Gendervision: Sexuality and Gender on Transatlantic Reality Television*, edited by Brenda Weber, 54–75. Durham, NC: Duke University Press, 2014.

Keats, John. *The Crack in the Picture Window*. New York: Houghton Mifflin, 1956.

Klein, Amanda Ann. "MTV Reality Programming and the Labor of Identity." *CST Online*, May 23, 2013. Available at: http://cstonline.tv/mtv. Accessed August 8, 2016.

Kraidy, Marwan, and Katherine Sender, eds. *The Politics of Reality Television: Global Perspectives*. New York: Routledge, 2011.

Kraszewski, Jon. "Country Hicks and Urban Cliques: Mediating Race, Reality, and Liberalism on MTV's The Real World." In *Reality TV: Remaking Television Culture*, 2nd edition, edited by Susan Murray and Laurie Ouellette, 205–22. New York: New York University Press, 2009.

Kraszewski, Jon. *The New Entrepreneurs: An Institutional History of Television Anthology Writers*. Middletown, CT: Wesleyan University Press, 2010.

Lee, Michael J., and Leigh Moscowitz. "The 'Ritch Bitch': Class and Gender on The Real Housewives of New York City." *Feminist Media Studies* 13, no. 1 (2013): 64–82.

Lefebvre, Henri. *The Production of Space*. Translated by Donald Nicholson-Smith. Malden, MA: Blackwell Publishing, 1991.

Levine, Lawrence. *Highbrow/Lowbrow: The Emergence of Cultural Hierarchy in America*. Cambridge, MA: Harvard University Press, 1990.

Lipsitz, George. *The Possessive Investment in Whiteness: How White People Profit from Identity Politics*, Revised edition. Philadelphia, PA: Temple University Press, 2006.

Lynch, Kevin. *The Image of the City*. Cambridge, MA: The MIT Press, 1960.

Maher, Jennifer. "What Do Women Watch?: Tuning In to the Compulsory Heterosexuality Channel." In *Reality TV: Remaking Television Culture*, 1st edition, edited by Susan Murray and Laurie Ouellette, 197–213. New York: New York University Press, 2004.

Marshall, Armina. "The Theatre Guild on Radio and Television." In *A Pictorial History of the Theatre Guild with Special Material from Lawrence Langer and Armina Marshall*, edited by Norman Nadel, 211–15. New York: Crown, 1969.

Marwick, Alice. *Status Update: Celebrity, Publicity, and Branding in the Social Media Age.* New Haven, CT: Yale University Press, 2015.

Massey, Doreen. *World City.* London: Polity, 2007.

McCarthy, Anna. "Stanley Milgram, Allen Funt, and Me: Postwar Social Science and the 'First Wave' of Reality TV." In *Reality TV: Remaking Television Culture,* 1st edition, edited by Susan Murray and Laurie Ouellette, 19–39. New York: New York University Press, 2004.

Mele, Christopher. *Selling the Lower East Side: Culture, Real Estate, and Resistance in New York City.* Minneapolis, MN: University of Minnesota Press, 2000.

Miller, Arthur. "Tragedy and the Common Man." In *The Theatre Essays of Arthur Miller,* edited by Robert A. Martin, 4–7. New York: Viking, 1977.

Mills, Brett. "What Does It Mean to Call Television 'Cinematic'?" In *Television Aesthetics and Style,* edited by Jason Jacobs and Steven Peacock, 57–66. New York: Bloomsbury, 2013.

Mills, C. Wright. *White Collar: The American Middle Classes.* New York: Oxford University Press, 1951.

Mittell, Jason. *Genre and Television: From Cop Shows to Cartoons in American Culture.* New York: Routledge, 2004.

Mittell, Jason. *Complex TV: The Poetics of Contemporary Television Storytelling.* New York: New York University Press, 2015.

Mulvey, Laura. *Visual and Other Pleasures.* Bloomington, IN: Indiana University Press, 1989.

Murphy, Kim. "Fairbanks Area, Trying to Stay Warm, Chokes on Wood Stove Pollution." *Los Angeles Times,* February 13, 2013. Available at: http://articles.latimes.com/2013/feb/16/nation/la-na-fairbanks-air-pollution-20130217. Accessed May 30, 2016.

Murray, Susan, and Laurie Ouellette, eds. *Reality TV: Remaking Television Culture,* 1st edition. New York: New York University Press, 2004.

Murray, Susan, and Laurie Ouellette, eds. *Reality TV: Remaking Television Culture,* 2nd edition. New York: New York University Press, 2009.

Naremore, James. *More Than Night: Film Noir in its Contexts.* Berkeley, CA: University of California Press, 1998.

Navarro, Mireya. "'Poor Door' in a New York Tower Opens a Fight Over Affordable Housing." *The New York Times,* August 26, 2014. Available at: http://www.nytimes.com/2014/08/27/nyregion/separate-entryways-for-new-york-condo-buyers-and-renters-create-an-affordable-housing-dilemma.html?_r=0. Accessed September 25, 2014.

Newman, Michael. *New York City English*. Berlin: De Gruyter Mouton, 2014.

Newman, Michael Z., and Elana Levine. *Legitimating Television: Media Convergence and Cultural Studies*. New York: Routledge, 2012.

Ouellette, Laurie, ed. *A Companion to Reality TV*. Malden, MA: Wiley-Blackwell, 2013.

Ouellette, Laurie, and James Hay. *Better Living through Reality TV: Television and Post-Welfare Citizenship*. Malden, MA: Wiley-Blackwell, 2008.

Owen, Rob. "Survivor Marks 10 Years with Heroes-Villains Showdown." *Pittsburgh Post-Gazette*, February 11, 2010. Available at: http://www.lexisnexis.com/hottopics/lnacademic#sthash.0UskD1Sg.dpuf. Accessed May 8, 2015.

Palmer, Gareth, ed. *Exposing Lifestyle Television*. London: Ashgate, 2008.

Peters, John Durham. "Nomadism, Diaspora, Exile: The Stakes of Mobility with the Western Canon." In *Home, Exile, Homeland: Film, Media, and the Politics of Place*, edited by Hamid Nacify, 17–44. New York: Routledge, 1999.

Pickens, Theri A. "Shoving Aside the Politics of Respectability: Black Women, Reality Television, and the Ratchet." *Women & Performance: A Journal of Feminist Theory* (2014): 1–18.

Pike, Kirsten. "Freaky Five-Year-Olds and Mental Mommies: Narratives of Gender, Race, and Class in TLC's Toddlers & Tiaras." In *Reality Gendervision: Sexuality & Gender on Transatlantic Reality Television*, edited by Brenda Weber, 282–98. Durham, NC: Duke University Press, 2014.

Puleo, Steve. *The Boston Italians: A Story of Pride, Perseverance, and Paesani, from the Years of the Great Immigration to the Present Day*. Boston, MA: Beacon, 2007.

Ramirez Berg, Charles. *Latino Images in Film: Stereotypes, Subversion, and Resistance*. Austin, TX: University of Texas Press, 2002.

Rapping, Elayne. "Aliens, Nomads, Mad Dogs, and Road Warriors: The Changing Face of Criminal Violence on TV." In *Reality TV: Remaking Television Culture*, 1st edition, edited by Susan Murray and Laurie Ouellette, 214–30. New York: New York University Press, 2004.

Reisman, David with Nathaniel Glazer and Reuel Denney. *The Lonely Crowd*. New Haven, CT: Yale University Press, 1950.

Rosen, Craig. "It Was 20 Years Ago Today: Two Decades On, VH1 Has Changed Its Tune Several Times—But the Beat Goes On and On. (VH1 at 20)." *The Hollywoodreporter.com*, September 27, 2005. Available at: http://www.lexisnexis.com/hottopics/lnacademic#sthash.0UskD1Sg.dpuf. Accessed September 30, 2012.

Rosen, Craig. "Music Man: New VH1 General Manager Tom Calderone Promises That Under His Watch, The Song Will Not Remain The Same." *The Hollywoodreporter.com*, September 27, 2005. Available at: http://www.lexisnexis.com/hottopics/lnacademic#sthash.0UskD1Sg.dpuf. Accessed September 30, 2012.

Rosensweig, Daniel. *Retro Ball Parks: Instant History, Baseball, and the New American City.* Knoxville, TN: University of Tennessee Press, 2005.

Ruoff, Jeffrey. *An American Family: A Televised Life.* Minneapolis, MN: University of Minnesota Press, 2002.

Ryden, Kent C. *Mapping the Invisible Landscape: Folklore, Writing, and a Sense of Place.* Iowa City, IA: University of Iowa Press, 1993.

Said, Edward. *Orientalism.* New York: Pantheon, 1978.

Saldanha, Arun. "Power Geometry as Philosophy of Space." In *Spatial Politics: Essays for Doreen Massey,* edited by David Featherstone and Joe Painter, 44–55. Malden, MA: Wiley-Blackwell, 2013.

Sampson, Harold, Sheldon L. Messinger, and Robert Towne. *Schizophrenic Women: Studies in Marital Crisis.* New York: Atherton Press, 1964.

Sassen, Saskia. *Cities in a World Economy,* 4th edition. London: Sage, 2012.

Sassen, Saskia. *Expulsions: Brutality and Complexity in the Global Economy.* Cambridge, MA: Harvard University Press, 2014.

Scharff, Virginia. *Taking the Wheel, Women and the Coming of the Motor Age.* Albuquerque, NM: University of New Mexico Press, 1992.

Sender, Katherine. "Real Worlds: Migrating Genres, Travelling Participants, Shifting Theories." In *The Politics of Reality Television: Global Perspectives,* edited by Marwan Kraidy and Katherine Sender, 1–11. New York: Routledge, 2011.

Sender, Katherine. *The Makeover: Reality TV and the Reflexive Audience.* New York: New York University Press, 2012.

Shields, Rob. *Places on the Margin: Alternative Geographies of Modernity.* New York: Routledge, 1991.

Sontag, Susan. "Notes on Camp." In *Camp: Queer Aesthetics and the Performing Subject: A Reader,* edited by Fabio Cleto, 53–65. Ann Arbor, MI: University of Michigan Press, 1999.

Starr, Michael. "Toddlers & Trash: TLC Has Built a Network on Exploitation—Is It Any Wonder Why It's Blowing Up in Their Face?" *New York Post,* May 24, 2015, 15.

Stern, Leonard B. "Marty, Broadway Hit, Written by Clintonite, '39." *Clinton News,* May 6, 1955.

Strachan, Alex. "Always Room for Reality Television: CBS Chief: But Moonves Warns Against Chasing Trends: Decision to Delay Beverly Hillbillies Reality Program Resulted From Senate Protests, He Tells Critics' Group." *The Gazette* (Montreal, QC), July 21, 2003.

Turow, Joseph. *Breaking Up America: Advertisers and the New Media World.* Chicago, IL: University of Chicago Press, 1997.

Valdivia, Angharad N. *Latina/os and the Media.* Malden, MA: Polity, 2010.

Wang, Hansi Lo. "Fuhgeddaboudit: New York Accent on its Way Out, Linguists Say." NPR.org, February 2, 2015. Available at: http://www.npr.org/2015/02/02/383289958/fuhgeddaboudit-new-york-accent-on-its-way-out-linguists-say. Accessed December 10, 2015.

Ward, Jervette R. "The Real Scandal: Portrayals of Black Women in Reality TV." In *Real Sister: Stereotypes, Respectability, and Black Women in Reality TV,* edited by Jervette R. Ward, 1–15. New Brunswick, NJ: Rutgers University Press, 2015.

Ward, Jervette R., ed. *Real Sister: Stereotypes, Respectability, and Black Women in Reality TV.* New Brunswick, NJ: Rutgers University Press, 2015.

Warren, Carol A.B. *Madwives: Schizophrenic Women in the 1950s.* New Brunswick, NJ: Rutgers University Press, 1987.

Watts, Amber. "Melancholy, Merit, and Merchandise: The Postwar Audience Participation Show." In *Reality TV: Remaking Television Culture,* 2nd edition, edited by Susan Murray and Laurie Ouellette, 301–20. New York: New York University Press, 2009.

Weber, Brenda. *Makeover TV: Selfhood, Citizenship, and Celebrity.* Durham, NC: Duke University Press, 2009.

Weber, Brenda. "Introduction: Trash Talk: Gender as an Analytic on Reality Television." In *Reality Gendervision: Sexuality & Gender on Transatlantic Reality Television,* edited by Brenda Weber, 1–34. Durham, NC: Duke University Press, 2014.

Weber, Brenda, ed. *Reality Gendervision: Sexuality & Gender on Transatlantic Reality Television.* Durham, NC: Duke University Press, 2014.

Wells, Ken, Aaron Kurlioff, and Charles R. Babvock. "Oil Spills in Most Imperiled U.S. Coastal Wetland Escapes Fines." *Bloomberg Business Review,* February 3, 2011. Available at: http://www.bloomberg.com/news/articles/2011-02-03/oil-spills-in-most-imperiled-u-s-coastal-wetland-escape-fines. Accessed May 30, 2016.

Whyte, Jr., William H. *The Organization Man.* New York: Doubleday, 1957.

Williams, Raymond. *The Country and the City.* New York: Oxford University Press, 1973.

Williams, Raymond. *Marxism and Literature.* New York: Oxford University Press, 1978.

Yarbrough, Marilyn, and Crystal Bennett. "Cassandra and the Sistahs: The Peculiar Treatment of African American Women in the Myth of the Liars." *Journal of Gender, Race, and Justice* (Spring 2000): 626–57.

VIDEOGRAPHY

The following list is not exhaustive, but it does offer the title, dates, production company, channel, and a brief description of the reality shows discussed in this book. I have also included additional titles of reality shows that shot people in real urban and rural spaces and touched on themes addressed in my book. With the ubiquity of reality shows on television, one of the best ways to research the genre further is to go to channel websites and peruse their shows.

19 Kids and Counting (2009–15). Figure 8 Films. TLC. Freakshow TLC reality show.
Alaska: The Last Frontier (2011–present). Discovery Studios. Discovery Channel. Rural reality show.
The Amazing Race (2001–present). Earthview Inc., Bruckheimer Television, Touchstone Television. CBS. Reality gameshow.
America's Castles (1998–2005). Cinetel Productions. A & E. Documents homes and castles of America's elite.
America's Funniest Home Videos (1990–present). ABC Entertainment, Vin Di Bona Productions. Home video show.
An American Family (1973). WNET New York. PBS. First-wave reality show.
American Ninja Warrior (2009–present). A. Smith & Co. Productions. NBC. Reality gameshow set in cities.
Animal Cops: Houston (2003–12, 2014–present). ITV Studios. Animal Planet. Urban reality law show.

The Apprentice (2004–present). Mark Burnett Productions, United Artists Media Group, MGM Television. NBC. Reality gameshow.

The Apprentice: Martha Stewart (2005). Mark Burnett Productions. NBC. Reality gameshow.

The Bachelor (2002–present). Next Entertainment, Warner Bros. Television, Warner Horizon Television, Telepictures Productions. ABC. Reality dating show.

The Bachelorette (2003–present). Next Entertainment, Warner Horizon Television, Telepictures Productions. ABC. Reality dating show.

Baldwin Hills (2007–09). C4 Productions. BET. African American reality show about urban teens.

Basketball Wives (2010–13). Shed Media. VH1. African American reality show about wives of NBA players.

Bethany Ever After (2010–12). Shed Media. Bravo. Spin-off of *The Real Housewives of New York City*.

Billy the Exterminator (2009–12). September Films. A & E. Southern reality show.

Breaking Bonaduce (2005–07). 3Ball Productions. VH1. Celebrity reality show.

Buying Alaska (2012–15). Paper Route Productions. Destination America. Rural real estate show.

Buying Hawaii (2013–present). Paper Route Productions. Destination America. Real estate show.

Buzzkill (1996). MTV Productions. MTV. Hidden camera prank show.

Cake Boss (2009–present). High Noon Entertainment. TLC. Family business reality show.

Candid Camera (first run, 1948–67). Allen Funt Productions. ABC, NBC, CBS, Syndication. First wave reality prank show.

Chainsaw Gang (2012–present). A. Smith & Co. Productions. CMT. Rural reality show.

Cheaters (2000–present). Bobby Goldstein Productions, Inc. Syndication. Urban private detective reality show.

Chrisley Knows Best (2014–present). Maverick Television. All3Media America. USA. Atlanta reality show.

The City (2008–10). Done and Done Productions. MTV. Urban reality show.

COPS (1989–present). Fox Television Stations, 20th Century Fox Television, Langley Productions, Spike Original Productions. Fox and Spike. Reality law show.

Cowboy U (2003–07). Triage Entertainment. CMT. Rural reality show.

Daisy of Love (2009). 51 Minds Entertainment. VH1. Reality dating show.

Deadliest Catch (2005–present). Original Productions, Fremantle Media, Image Entertainment. Discovery Channel. Rural/Alaskan/fishing reality show.

Dog the Bounty Hunter (2004–12). Hybrid Films. A & E. Reality justice show set in Hawaii.

Duck Dynasty (2012–present). Gurney Productions. A & E. Rural reality show.

Flavor of Love (2006–08). 51 Minds Entertainment. VH1. Reality dating show.

Flavor of Love: Charm School (2007). 51 Minds Entertainment. VH1. Reality game show.

Flip This House (2005–09). Departure Films. A & E. Reality real estate show.

Flipping Boston (2013–14). Departure Films. A & E. Reality real estate show.

Flipping Out (2007–present). Authentic Entertainment. Bravo. Reality real estate show.

Frank the Entertainer: A Basement Affair (2010). 51 Minds Entertainment. VH1. Reality dating show.

Gigolos (2011–present). RelativityReal. Showtime. Reality dating show with paid escorts.

God, Guns, & Automobiles (2013). Zone3. History. Rural reality show.

Gold Rush (2010–present). Raw Television. Discovery Channel. Rural reality show.

Guntucky (2013–present). Leftfield Pictures. CMT. Rural reality show.

Here Comes Honey Boo (2012–14). Authentic Entertainment. TLC. Rural reality show.

The Hills (2006–10). Done and Done Productions. MTV. Urban reality show.

Hogan Knows Best (2005–07). Pink Sneakers Productions. VH1. Celebrity reality show.

House Hunters (1999–present). Pie Town Productions. Reality real estate show.

I Love Money (2008–10). 51 Minds Entertainment. Reality game show.

I Love New York (2007–08). 51 Minds Entertainment. Reality dating show.

Ice Road Truckers (2007–present). Original Productions, Prospero Media, Shaw Media. A & E. Rural reality show.

Jon and Kate Plus 8 (2007–09). Figure 8 Films, Advanced Medical Productions. Discovery Health and TLC. Freakshow TLC reality show.

Juiced (2006). Pay-Per-View reality prank show with O.J. Simpson that never aired. There are 200 or so DVD copies in circulation now.

Keeping Up With The Kardashians (2007–present). Ryan Seacrest Productions, Bunim/Murray Productions. Urban reality show.

Kourtney and Khloe Take Miami (2009–10). Ryan Seacrest Productions, Bunim/Murray Productions. Urban reality show.

Kourtney and Kim Take Miami (2013). Ryan Seacrest Productions, Bunim/Murray Productions. Urban reality show.

Kourtney and Kim Take New York (2011–12). Ryan Seacrest Productions, Bunim/Murray Productions. Urban reality show.

LA Ink (2007–11). Original Media. TLC. Urban reality show.

The Little Couple (2009–present). LMNO Productions. TLC. Freakshow TLC reality show.

Love and Hip Hop (2011–present). Monami Entertainment. VH1. African American reality show about wives of hip hop artists.

Married at First Sight (2014–present). Kinetic Content. FYI and A & E. Reality marriage show.

Megan Wants a Millionaire (2009). 51 Minds Entertainment. Realty dating show.

Miami Ink (2005–08). Original Media. TLC. Urban reality show

The Millionaire Matchmaker (2008–15). Bayonne Entertainment, Intuitive Entertainment. Bravo. Reality dating show.

Moonshiners (2011–present). Maglia Entertainment. Discovery Channel. Rural reality show.

My 600 Pound Life (2012–present). Megalomedia. TLC. Freakshow TLC reality show.

My Big Fat Fabulous Life (2015–present). Pilgrim Studios. TLC. Freakshow TLC reality show.

My Big Redneck Wedding (2008–11). Pink Sneakers Productions. CMT. Rural reality show.

My Fair Brady (2005–08). 51 Minds Entertainment. VH1 Celebrity reality show.

New York Goes to Hollywood (2008). 51 Minds Entertainment. VH1. Urban reality show.

New York Goes to Work (2009). 51 Minds Entertainment. VH1. Urban reality show.

NY Ink (2011–13). Original Media. TLC. Urban reality show.

The Osbornes (2002–05). Big Head Productions. MTV. Family reality show.

Our Little Family (2015–present). Discovery Studios. TLC. Freakshow TLC reality show.

Parking Wars (2008–12). Hyrbid Films. A & E. Urban reality show.

Pitbulls and Parolees (2009–present). 44 Blue Productions. Animal Planet. Family business reality show.

Punk'd (2002–07, 2012, 2015–present). Rogue Atlas Productions, Lionsgate. MTV, BET. Hidden camera prank show.

Real Chance at Love (2009). 51 Minds Entertainment. VH1. Reality dating show.

The Real Housewives of Atlanta (2008–present). Evolution Media. Bravo. Urban reality show.

The Real Housewives of Beverly Hills (2010–present). Evolution Media. Bravo. Urban reality show.

The Real Housewives of Dallas (2016–present). Evolution Media. Bravo. Urban reality show.

The Real Housewives of Miami (2011–13). Evolution Media. Bravo. Urban reality show.

The Real Housewives of New Jersey (2009–present). Evolution Media. Bravo. Urban reality show.

The Real Housewives of New York City (2008–present). Evolution Media. Bravo. Urban reality show.

The Real Housewives of Orange County (2006–present). Evolution Media. Bravo. Urban reality show.

The Real Housewives of Potomac (2016–present). Evolution Media. Bravo. Urban reality show.

The Real Housewives of Washington, DC (2010). Evolution Media. Bravo. Urban reality show.

The Real World (1992–present). Bunim/Murray Productions. MTV. Urban reality show.

Rehab Addict (2010–present). Magnetic Productions. DIY, HGTV. Reality real estate show.

Rock of Love (2007–09). 51 Minds Entertainment. VH1. Reality dating show.

Selling Los Angeles (2011–present). JV Productions Inc. HGTV. Reality real estate show.

Selling New York (2010–present). JV Productions Inc. HGTV. Reality real estate show.

Spartan: Ultimate Team Challenge (2016). A. Smith & Company. NBC. Reality game show set in rural Georgia.

Steven Seagal: Lawman (2009–14). ITV Studios, Steamroller Films. A & E, Reelz. Reality cop show.

The Surreal Life (2003–06). 51 Minds Entertainment. The WB, VH1. Celebrity reality show.

Survivor (2000–present). Survivor Production LLC, Castaway Television Productions, Mark Burnett Productions, One Three Media, United Artists Media Group, MGM Television. CBS. Reality gameshow.

Swamp People (2010–present). Original Media. History. Rural reality show.

Temptation Island (2001–03). Fox World. Fox. Reality dating show.

Toddlers and Tiaras (2009–present). Authentic Entertainment. TLC. Freakshow TLC reality show.

Vanderpump Rules (2013–present). Evolution Media. Bravo. Urban reality show.

Wahlburgers (2014–present). 44 Blue Productions. A & E. Urban reality show.

INDEX